CORFU

POCKET GUIDE

ARTS & CULTURE

Space disco ho...
featuring the...

A TO Z INFO

SHOPPING

Shopping in...
around in...
be foun...
— with...

DIAMANT
Restaurant

BROOKLAWN

JOE'S BURGERS

Charcoal Broiled STEAKS

100 m

100 m

GATE BRIDGE

MAP

SHARE

LIKE

100 m

Sailing under the Golden Gate Bridge today, it is interesting to consider that engineers once thought it impossible to span the Golden Gate Strait at this point, because of the depth of the water (318ft/ 97 meters, at its deepest point) and the power ful tidal rush.

The city authorized studies for a bridge in 1917, but it was 1933 before the first shovel turned under the gaze of master engineer Joseph B. Strauss (no relation to the famous waltz composer). Four years later the bridge opened, at a cost of \$35 million and the lives of 11 construction workers. Today the bridge

INSIGHT GUIDES
SPAIN

INTRODUCTION

EXPLORE B...

EXP...

FLORIDA

This new edition of Insight Guide Florida is comprehensive, full-colour travel guide packed with inspiration and... information. It includes everything...

FRANCE

This brand new edition Insight Guide to France features outstanding full-colour photography with...

ST LUCIA Pocket Guide

 **Walking Eye**
mobile app

Discover the world's best destinations with the Insight Guides Walking Eye app, available to download for free in the App Store and Google Play.

The container app provides easy access to fantastic free content on events and activities taking place in your current location or chosen destination, with the possibility of booking, as well as the regularly-updated Insight Guides travel blog: Inspire Me. In addition, you can purchase curated, premium destination guides through the app, which feature local highlights, hotel, bar, restaurant and shopping listings, an A to Z of practical information and more. Or purchase and download Insight Guides eBooks straight to your device.

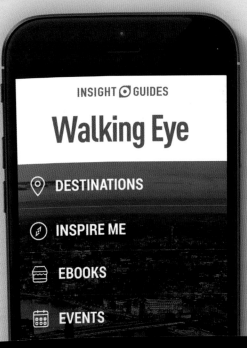

TOP 10 ATTRACTIONS

THE NORTHEAST COAST
This part of Corfu is particularly beautiful, with pebble coves and striking mountain scenery. See page 60.

THE WEST COAST
Noted for its glorious sandy beaches, including Glyfáda and Kondogialós. See page 72.

PALEOKASTRÍTSA
The island's most famous beauty spot. See page 69.

PAXÍ AND ANDÍPAXI
Take a day trip to this delightful island and its tiny satellite. See page 76.

ANGELÓKASTRO
The medieval fortress offers sweeping views. See page 71.

LISTÓN
The elegant promenade was modelled on the Rue de Rivoli in Paris. See page 33.

BYZANTINE MUSEUM
It houses a fine collection of icons painted by refugee Cretan masters settled on Corfu. See page 36.

ARCHAEOLOGICAL MUSEUM
The massive Gorgon pediment dominates this Kérkyra Town attraction. See page 44.

MUSEUM OF ASIAN ART
Unexpected, world-class collection in Kérkyra Town. See page 32.

ACHILLEION PALACE
This grandiosely kitsch building is one of the most visited sights on the island. See page 50.

A PERFECT TOUR

Day 1

Corfu Town

Start with a coffee at a café on the Listón. Cross the Spianáda to take in the Paleó Froúrio, then marvel at the Asian Art and Archaeological museums. After lunch, climb the Néo Froúrio, then head out to Glyfáda or Kondogialós for a swim. Watch the sunset from the Kaiser's Throne at Pélekas. Return to town for dinner.

Day 2

The south

On your way south, stop at the Paleópolis museum, then visit the Achilleion. Have lunch at Boúkari Beach or Alonaki Bay tavernas, then spend the afternoon on the beach – Íssos has dunes, Agía Varvára is more child-friendly. Try Klimataria in Benítses, or Venetian Well in Kérkyra Town, for supper.

Day 3

The northeast

Head northeast from town, pausing to visit the National Gallery Annexe in Káto Korakiána. Then have lunch at Agní, Kouloúra or Ágios Stéfanos. Kamináki and Kerasiá have the best pebble beaches in the area. In the evening, drive up to Paleá Períthia for dinner in the old village square. Change your overnight base to Kassiópi, Róda or Aharávi with tomorrow's trip in mind.

Day 4

Eríkoussa

Hop on a boat in Róda or Sidári for a daytrip to Eríkousa, the closest of the Diapóndia islets. Then head to Perouládes to watch the sunset from the cliffs over Longás beach. Be sure to pre-book a stay at Delfino Blu Hotel in Ágios Stéfanos Gýrou, or arrange to have dinner at their gourmet restaurant.

OF **CORFU**

Day 7

Round-up

Today, catch whatever you've missed so far. Try the Patounis Soap Factory just off Sarroko Square; the nearby Scuola Greca synagogue, the main remnant of the Jewish community destroyed in 1944; or the Folklore Museum in Sinarádes. Have lunch in town at Mouragia for views of Vídos islet and some sea breeze, or tuck into seafood at Roulas's, overlooking Gouviá yacht port. Finally, take an excursion boat from the old port to Vídos, with its decent beach and cenotaph for the Serbs expired here in 1916. Have a final dinner at Salto Wine Bar, also at the old port.

Day 5

Northwest

Start the day at magnificent Ágios Geórgios Págon beach, with lunch at Akrogiali taverna towards the south end of the bay. Then head to the castle of Angelókastro for its views over Paleokastrítsa, your late-afternoon destination – perhaps another swim before visiting the lovely Theotókou monastery towards dusk. Have dinner in Doukádes village, at Elizabeth's (see page 112), before an overnight close to Kérkyra's new port.

Day 6

Paxí and Andípaxi

Take a day cruise to these two islets south of Corfu. Likely targets will be the Paxiot west coast with its spectacular Orthólithos stack and sea caves which the boat enters, or the mock-Caribbean coves lining Andípaxi's northeast coast. Dinner in return in Kérkyra Town – perhaps at La Famiglia (see page 105) for some Italian fare.

CONTENTS

INTRODUCTION

Swathed in a blanket of deep green vegetation, its mountainous skyline subsiding into a crystal-clear, turquoise sea, Corfu is known as Greece's Emerald Island. It is not only among the lushest of Greece's myriad islands, but one of the prettiest as well. Flowering shrubs and trees cloak most of its rolling landscape, and in spring the island explodes in a beautiful wildflower display.

Corfu's sunny beaches, spectacular scenery and charming capital have enchanted visitors – including many writers and artists – through the centuries. The wonderful clear light and stunning vistas of the island are thought to have been the inspiration for settings in Homer's *Odyssey* and Shakespeare's *The Tempest*. In more recent times, the British writer and painter Edward Lear depicted many views of Corfu's now famous sights, while the authors Lawrence and Gerald Durrell both lived here and wrote entertaining books about island life.

SECLUDED RESORTS

Since the late 1970s, Corfu has become a popular British playground; for many years over half of the island's holiday visitors came from the UK. No doubt early visitors felt at home in Kérkyra Town (Corfu Town) sipping ginger beer and watching cricket matches – both relics of British rule (1814–64) that can still be enjoyed today. The introduction of cheap package tourism in the 1980s gave Corfu something of a reputation as

All Greek to me

Language is no problem for most visitors. Many locals speak English or Italian, and most signs are posted in both Greek and Roman characters.

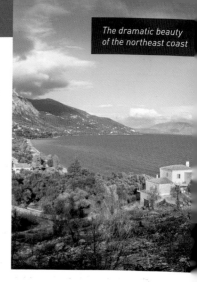

a 'party island'. However, the party scene was always restricted to a few enclaves, and since the millennium some of those have mellowed considerably. Nonetheless, there are definitely still a few places that are best avoided by anyone who prefers the atmosphere of a Greek island to a rowdy British seaside town. Lately, however, numbers of central/eastern Europeans – Poles, Serbs, Russians, Czechs, Romanians and Bulgarians –plus Israelis, have risen sharply.

In keeping with island character and scale, many resorts are small, quiet and secluded. Though development has been rapid on some parts of Corfu, it is still much less overbearing than in many other Mediterranean vacation destinations. There is only one high-rise horror (at Barbáti) and only the occasional large hotel, and actually, much of the island remains untouched by mass tourism. The main resorts are really crowded only in July and August and remarkably, even in peak season you can still find secluded places for sunbathing and hiking. You just have to make an extra effort (usually on foot or by boat) to get there.

LOCATION AND SIZE

Corfu is the most northerly of the Ionian group of islands. Just across the water to the east are Albania and the Greek mainland. Italy lies only 40 nautical miles to the northwest.

The Listón, Kérkyra (Corfu) Town

To the south are delightful Paxí and the other Ionian islands (Lefkáda, Itháki, Kefaloniá, Zákynthos and Kýthira). However, island-hopping here is an option only for travellers with lots of time on their hands; it involves travel via the mainland.

Corfu is also Greece's western gateway and has proudly styled itself 'the entry to the Adriatic'. It is telling that the Ottomans – who conquered the rest of mainland Greece and Lefkáda among the Ionian Islands – failed to gain a foothold here. Instead, it was the great Western European powers of the day (Venice, France and Britain) that left their mark during five centuries of island occupation. Nowhere is this more noticeable than in the elegant architecture and cosmopolitan atmosphere of Kérkyra Town. Where else in the world could you sit at a French-style café, amid Venetian streets, sipping Greek coffee while gazing at an English palace? This stylish capital is regarded as the loveliest town in all the Greek islands, and a visit here is a highlight of most visitors' holidays.

In its shape Corfu resembles a scythe, measuring about 65km (40 miles) in length and ranging in width from 4km to 30km (2.5 miles to 19 miles). The island is the exposed crown of a submerged mountain range that broke off from the mainland to the east aeons ago. The highest point is Mt Pandokrátor, only a relatively modest peak of 914m (2,999ft), but on this relatively small island it takes on much more importance, and the summit is reached by an impressive ascent along steep hairpin bends.

Hire a car, if only for a few days, as you can very easily get around and explore the whole island. As you tour Corfu you'll see undulating hills and stone terraces bordered by silvery groves of prized olive trees – venerable and gnarled. In the past they were an economic lifeline for the island, and still provide excellent olive oil and wood. The island is also graced with groves of kumquat and lemon trees (giving off a glorious aroma in spring), plane trees, jacaranda, palms, wisteria, myrtle and oleander. Even the simplest homes are adorned with verdant grape arbours and enormous, beautiful clusters of roses or bougainvillea. Most memorable of all are the groves of tall, slim cypresses rising like sentries on the hillsides.

Visit in spring or early summer, if possible, to see the best of the island's flora: there are 100 native wild flowers alone that grow nowhere else. You might get a little wet then, but it's a price worth paying. The reason for Corfu's remarkably luxuriant vegetation is that more rain falls here – deflected by the nearby mainland mountains – than in any other part of Greece: typically 1m (39.4in) between October and June. However, during mid-summer this is very much an island in the sun.

CLEAN BEACHES, CASUAL LIVING

Corfu has about 200km (125 miles) of coastline with some of Europe's most beautiful and cleanest beaches. They vary from

strips of pure golden sand to fine pea-gravel or bright white pebbles, and combinations of all three. While swells for surfing can be found on the western shores, there are plenty of calm bays suitable for all the family on the more protected east coast. As for the sea itself, in any one cove the range of clear blues seems to defy the colour spectrum. Don't miss a day trip to the Diapóndia islets or Andípaxi, where the waters are as clear as those in the Caribbean.

Around 120,000 people live on Corfu. Some emigrate – attracted by life abroad or in the big mainland cities – but many never leave the island. Instead, the world comes to them, in increasing numbers that today reach one million annually. Yet despite the seasonal influx of visitors, the inhabitants on the whole retain a fresh, open simplicity that delights visitors.

Life on Corfu is casual and unhurried. For the punctilious northern European visitor it can sometimes be a bit too casual: waiting for a bus that is 20 minutes late (or never comes); the 'fast-food' souvláki, for which you have to queue for 15 minutes; the restaurant order that takes an eternity to arrive cold. Be patient and remember that nobody ever came to Corfu (or anywhere else in Greece, for that matter) for swift service, gourmet French food or impeccable plumbing. After all, the slow pace of life here is intrinsic to Greece's appeal for most visitors.

A BRIEF HISTORY

Little is known about Corfu's first inhabitants. Prehistoric traces found at Gardíki in the southwest date back to the Middle Palaeolithic Era (c.40,000 BC), when the island was probably joined to the Greek mainland. Unlike on other Ionian islands, however, no traces of Mycenaean settlements have ever surfaced on Corfu, which may instead have been held by the Phoenicians during the late Bronze Age (1500 BC to 1150 BC).

Corfu's acknowledged history begins in 734 BC, when the Corinthians established a colony called Korkyra, south of today's Kérkyra Town, in an area known as Paleópolis (Old City). Archaeological digs (still in progress) have turned up temples near Kardáki Spring and Mon Repos, but the ancient city was otherwise destroyed by barbarian raiders and its stone masonry subsequently used to build medieval Kérkyra Town. The famous, early-6th-century BC Gorgon pediment from the Temple of Artemis, now in the Archaeological Museum, is the most important surviving artefact of classical Korkyra.

Prospering from trade with southern Italy, Korkyra grew into a strong maritime power. In 665 BC, Korkyra defeated Corinth in what the historian Thucydides described as the first naval battle in Greek history, thus gaining independence and subsequently founding colonies of her own. Corfu's pact with Athens against Corinth and Sparta in 433 BC proved to be, according to Thucydides, the final straw that set off the Peloponnesian War and hastened the end of classical Greece.

From then on, Corfu suffered attack, pillage and often highly destructive occupation. Situated barely a nautical mile from the Epirot mainland at its nearest point, Corfu's safe harbours, fertile soil and strategic position between the Adriatic and Ionian seas made it a prize worth contesting by any power aiming to control the region.

ROMAN CONQUEST, BARBARIAN RAIDS

Around 229 BC a Roman fleet arrived and seized the island from the Illyrian queen Teuta, making Corfu the Roman republic's earliest Adriatic conquest. For the next five and a half centuries, Corfu prospered as a Roman naval base. En route to and from battles Nero, Tiberius, Cato, Cicero, Caesar, Octavian and Mark Antony (with Cleopatra) were among the Roman notables who visited Corfu. During the 1st century AD two saints – Iason (Jason) and Sosipatros (Sosipater) – brought Christianity to the island. Certain structures at Paleópolis are among the few remnants from Corfu's Roman period.

When the Roman Empire split in the 4th century AD, its eastern half, Byzantium, took administrative control of Corfu but could provide little security. Rampaging Vandals raided the island in AD 445, while in AD 562 a horde of Ostrogoths badly damaged Corfu's ancient capital. which, however, was only slowly abandoned from the 7th century onwards.

Partway through the 10th century, the Corfiots moved their capital 2km (1 mile) north and built their first fortress on the rocky bluff commanding the town's eastern sea approach. The Old Fort still stands today on this site. Elsewhere, islanders abandoned coastal settlements and retreated inland to establish protected hillside villages.

NORMANS AND SICILIANS

Then appeared a formidable new enemy. Several times between 1080 and 1185, Norman forces crossed the sea from

Sicily and Italy to attack Corfu and nearby outposts of the enfeebled Byzantine Empire. The rulers in Constantinople asked for help, the Venetians responded and thereafter took an active interest in the destiny of both Corfu and the empire as a whole.

When Doge Enrico Dandolo and his Fourth Crusade seized Constantinople in 1204, the spoils claimed by Venice included western Greece, parts

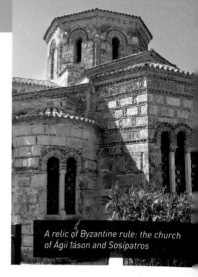

A relic of Byzantine rule: the church of Ágii Iáson and Sosípatros

of the Peloponnese and the Ionian islands. However, Venice was unable to extend immediate control over all its new possessions and Corfu aligned itself with the Greek Despotate of Epirus, which then held parts of what are today Albania and western Greece. In 1214 Mikhaïl Angelos Komnenos II, head of the despotate, formally acquired the island, strengthening existing fortresses at Angelókastro and Gardíki.

However, the Normans still had designs on Corfu. In 1259, the island was presented to King Manfred, the Hohenstaufen king of Sicily, as Mikhaïl's daughter Helena's dowry. Eight years later, the new king of Sicily and Naples, Charles d'Anjou, became the overlord of Corfu, where his family – the Angevins – subsequently ruled for over a century. During this time the traditional Eastern Orthodoxy of the island was almost extinguished by the new official religion of Roman Catholicism.

Mandráki swimming lido and yacht port

VENETIAN RULE

As Angevin power diminished, Corfu's fledgling assembly of 24 barons, mindful of the danger presented by marauding corsairs, invited Venice to send in a protective military force. The Venetians landed on 20 May 1386, beginning an uninterrupted occupation that lasted for over four centuries. In the following year, Corfu officially became part of the Stato da Màr, the Venetian maritime empire. Kérkyra Town prospered once again as a key port for galleys plying far-flung commercial routes, and the Venetians turned the Byzantine fort in Kérkyra Town into an impregnable bastion.

In 1463, having swept across mainland Greece, the Ottoman Turks declared war on Venice. During the following years they mounted many assaults on the Ionian Islands, and in 1537 they turned on Corfu. Intent on seizing Kérkyra Town, the Ottoman fleet, led by pirate-admiral Hayreddin Barbarossa landed cannon and 25,000 troops north of the capital at Gouviá. The fortress withstood a bitter attack, but the rest of the island was looted and the vengeful Turks carried off some 15,000 to 20,000 prisoners – nearly half the population – into slavery.

Following this great siege, the Venetians dug the Contrafossa, a canal separating the Old Fort from the town. They also erected a 'New Fortress' (so called even today) to guard the city's northwestern approach.

Corfu's finest military hour was to come in July 1716, once more against the Ottomans and once more at great cost. After losing both Athens and the Peloponnese to the Venetians late in the 17th century, the Ottomans successfully counterattacked, retaking the Peloponnese and Lefkáda before sending over 30,000 troops to besiege Corfu. Venice hired foreign regiments under the German mercenary commander Johann Matthias von der Schulenburg to defend the island. For five bloody weeks just 8,000 defenders held Kérkyra Town while the Ottomans, with their overwhelmingly superior forces, ravaged the rest of the island. They appeared poised to capture the capital when they suddenly called off their assault and fled, never to return, after severe casualties occasioned by a ferocious storm in August.

Throughout its long occupation, Venice kept Corfu under a strict feudal regime, a colony valued as an important naval base, trading depot and tariff-collection station. A civil-military governor and senior bureaucrats sent from Venice ran the island. Much like Venice's Libro d'Oro, a Golden Book listing the Corfiot nobility contained 277 families when Corfu passed from Venice to Napoleonic forces.

However, ordinary islanders were heavily taxed and denied public education, and Greek Orthodoxy was eclipsed by Roman Catholicism. Italian replaced Greek as the official language, even though the peasantry couldn't understand it and had no way of learning it. Many laboured

Patron saint

It is said that at the height of the Ottoman siege of August 1716, St Spyridon appeared amidst a raging storm with a lighted torch and scared the invaders away. August 11 is now one of the days that commemorate Corfu's patron saint (see page 38).

as serfs in the Venetian aristocrats' villas, some of which still dot the countryside.

More happily, Venice was responsible for nearly all the olive trees that grace Corfu's landscape. Olive production transformed the island's economy for good. Apart from the olive trees, the most visible legacies of Venetian rule are the older districts of Kérkyra Town: with its narrow streets and tall buildings, it is the most European city in Greece.

NAPOLEON'S DREAM ISLAND

In 1797 the doges' republic and its possessions fell to Napoleon through the Treaty of Campo Formio, thus ending 411 years

⊘ THE FIRST EUROPEAN

Corfu's most famous son is Ioannis Kapodistrias (1776–1831). Born into an aristocratic family, he became Greece's first president in 1827 and is hailed as the first statesman to envisage a unified Europe. From 1799 until 1807, Kapodistrias was instrumental in the administration of the Septinsular Republic under Russian tutelage. He then served until 1822 as a diplomat in the service of Russian Tsar Alexander I. On a mission to Switzerland in 1813, he orchestrated the Swiss Federation, which has endured to this day. Subsequently he began to develop ideas of a unified Europe in which no one member would become too powerful and in which the powers would collectively regulate the whole. In this vision he was a man ahead of his time. Sadly, his political ideals also attracted parochial enemies, and he was assassinated on the Greek mainland in 1831 by two clan chieftains. In 1994 his home island fittingly hosted a summit meeting of the very union of which he had dreamed.

of Venetian occupation. For reasons that remain obscure, Napoleon was rather obsessed with Corfu. 'The greatest misfortune which could befall me is the loss of Corfu,' he wrote rather melodramatically to his foreign minister, Talleyrand, and quickly sent a force to occupy Corfu and the other Ionian Islands.

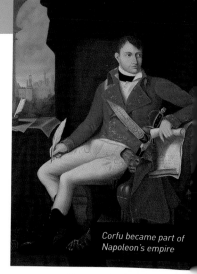

Corfu became part of Napoleon's empire

Napoleonic forces replaced Venice's autocratic rule with new democratic representation, burned Corfu's Golden Book, introduced public education and made Greek the official language. Nevertheless, they still managed to antagonise the island's inhabitants by continuing to suppress the Orthodox Church. Within two years the French were driven out of the island by a joint Russo-Ottoman force that reinstated Greek Orthodoxy as the official religion under the puppet 'Septinsular Republic'. However, in 1807 the French regained Corfu from the Russians by the Treaty of Tilsit. This time Napoleon garrisoned the citadels with 50,000 men along with 500 new cannon, making Corfu one of the most powerfully fortified points in the eastern Mediterranean.

The French also established the first Ionian Academy for the promotion of arts and sciences, imported Greece's first printing presses, drew up a street plan for Corfu Town, built a miniature Rue de Rivoli (the Listón) and introduced the cultivation of potatoes and tomatoes, now mainstays of Corfiot cooking.

Palace of St Michael and St George

THE BRITISH MOVE IN

After Napoleon's defeat at Waterloo, the British took Corfu in 1814 by the terms of the Treaty of Vienna, which turned the seven Ionian Islands into a notional state under British 'protection'. Corfu became the capital and Sir Thomas Maitland was appointed the first Lord High Commissioner.

The British occupation of Corfu lasted for just 50 years, and brought certain benefits. Under Maitland, a road network was built. His successor, Frederick Adam, built the road to Paleokastrítsa and brought a permanent water-supply system to Kérkyra Town. While some changes were mere personal caprice on the part of the ten British high commissioners, they also introduced hospitals, a model prison, a decent judiciary, and religious freedom, ensuring the primacy of the Orthodox Church. The slightly eccentric Frederic North, 5th Earl of Guilford – a philhellene who went about in Classical Greek dress and actually converted to Orthodox Christianity – established modern Greece's first university, the second Ionian Academy, in Kérkyra Town in 1824. He bequeathed to it his library of 25,000 books, thus making Corfu the country's chief literary and intellectual centre of that era.

The constitution set in place by Maitland was another matter. Though maintaining a façade of parliamentary government with a Corfiot senate and assembly, the high commissioner retained all effective power, despite token reforms during the 1830s. Serious unrest first occurred in the 1820s, when Maitland stopped the Corfiots from giving assistance to Greek mainlanders engaged in the war of independence against Turkey. This engendered bitterness among the islanders, who dubbed Maitland '*éktroma* (the abortion)' for his rudeness, and aversion to bathing.

GREEK AT LAST

When Prince William of Denmark was crowned King George I in Athens in 1864, Corfu and the six other Ionian Islands were ceded to Greece as a condition of George's accession to the throne. The islands were declared 'perpetually neutral', and, before hauling down the Union Jack, the British blew up the impressive fortifications they had added to Kérkyra Town. When they sailed off, the island's assembly made known its gratitude to Queen Victoria for this unprecedented voluntary withdrawal by a great power from an overseas possession.

Peace settled on the island in its early years as a province of Greece. Aristocratic tourists converged here, including Empress Elisabeth of Austria, who liked it so much that she commissioned the grandiose Achilleion Palace.

Although royalist Greece was officially neutral during the first three years of World War I, Venezelist-republican Corfu effectively served as an Allied military and naval base. In early 1916 Corfu gave refuge to the exiled government of Serbia and its troops as they fled defeat at the hands of the Bulgarians and Austrians. Thousands died from

The British legacy

The British left behind a number of stately buildings and monuments as well as cricket, ginger beer and Christmas chutney – island favourites even today.

wounds and disease, buried both on Vídos islet and at sea adjacent, but many more recovered at camps across the island, beginning a long-standing mutual love affair between Serbia and Corfu. On 31 August 1923 Mussolini ordered his fleet to bombard the island in reprisal for the murder of four high-ranking Italian officers on the Albanian-Greek border. Italian forces occupied Corfu for most of September until League of Nations mediations saw their withdrawal in exchange for a Greek apology and payment of reparations. The Italians returned as occupiers during World War II, from spring 1941 until Italy capitulated in September 1943.

When the Germans tried to succeed their defeated allies, the Italian troops (who had now switched sides) resisted on Corfu and throughout the Ionian islands. In the ensuing battles and bombardments, nearly a quarter of Kérkyra Town was destroyed, including the parliament house, academy and municipal theatre. After a year of occupation, during which the thriving Jewish community was deported to its death, German forces evacuated Corfu in October 1944, replaced by the British.

Corfu was largely unaffected by the Greek civil war between communist and royalist armies that raged on the mainland between 1947 and 1949, though in light of its rebellious republican past it was garrisoned by a special gendarmerie until the 1970s. Since then, tourism, real estate sales and agriculture – the three economic mainstays of the island – have brought unprecedented prosperity to much of Corfu, though it has been affected by the 2010–18 Greek debt crisis. It was strongly pro-SYRIZA in the 2015 elections but in July 2019 swung back to centre-right Néa Dimokratía under its new leader Kyriakos Mitsotakis, currently Greek prime minister with an absolute majority – the first non-coalition government since 2009.

HISTORICAL LANDMARKS

734 BC Corinthians found colony of Korkyra.

665 BC Korkyra gains independence, becomes Athenian ally.

229 BC – AD 336 Romans control Corfu, their first Adriatic colony.

336 AD Corfu becomes part of Byzantine Empire.

562 Ostrogoths devastate ancient Korkyra and its monuments.

933 Byzantine Corfiots establish new capital and build first fortress.

1185 Norman Angevins seize Corfu after several attempts.

1386 Venice acquires Corfu.

1537 Kérkyra Town withstands first Ottoman siege, but the country-side is sacked.

1572–1645 Venice erects great city walls and fortresses at Kérkyra.

1716 Corfiots, Venetians and allies repel final Ottoman siege.

1797 Napoleonic French acquire Ionian Islands from Venice.

1799 Russians and Ottomans seize Corfu; 'Septinsular Republic' set up.

1807–14 Ionian Islands again taken by Napoleonic French.

1814–64 Corfu becomes a British protectorate.

1831 Mainland Greece wins independence from Ottomans.

1864 Britain cedes Ionian Islands to Greece.

1916 Corfu gives refuge to exiled Serbian government and army.

1941 Corfu surrenders to Italy.

1943 Kérkyra Town damaged by Nazi bombardment as they occupy Corfu.

2007 Corfu's Old Town designated a Unesco World Heritage site.

2010–12 Greek debt becomes unmanageable; Greece goes under IMF/EU supervision.

2012–2015 Harsh austerity measures trigger political crises.

2015 Alexis Tsipras, leader of leftist party SYRIZA, becomes PM; international creditors grant Greece a third bailout after Tsipras caves to their demands.

2018–19 Greece emerges from financial supervision; in July 2019 elections, New Democracy regains power.

Corfu's colourful skyline

WHERE TO GO

Although Kérkyra Town (Corfu Town) is the heart and soul of the island, like most capitals it is not very representative. Unless you are travelling independently or just visiting Corfu briefly, it is unlikely that you will stay overnight in Kérkyra Town.

The vast majority of Corfu's visitors are on package tours and stay on the coast at accommodation ranging from modest apartments to luxury complexes. Nonetheless, Kérkyra Town acts as a magnet for shoppers, culture vultures, or the merely curious, and it rarely disappoints. Located about halfway down the east coast, it is within striking distance of any spot on the island and makes a useful reference point for us to begin our island tour.

We shall divide this tour as follows:

The South. The long, narrow southern portion of the island is often described (usually by people who haven't been to Corfu) as nothing more than a party zone. This is certainly true of its extremity (Kávos) but is not the case when applied to the whole area. The Achilleion Palace is Corfu's most-visited cultural attraction, while the long laid-back beaches of Ágios Geórgios Argyrádon and peaceful fishing villages such as Boúkari provide a sharp contrast to the busy resorts of Benítses, Moraïtika and Mesongí.

North of Kérkyra Town. Immediately north of the capital is the most developed part of the island. Its resorts are mostly hidden from the main road, occupying the large bays and inlets on this stretch of coastline.

The Northeast. Look at any website or brochure for expensive Corfu villas and you will find most are in the small area between Barbáti and Kassiópi. The Durrells made Kalámi the most famous resort on this stretch, but there are many similar ones nestling in

Enjoying an afternoon chat

the exquisite tiny coves that constitute 'Kensington-on-Sea'. A short distance inland looms Mt Pandokrátor.

The North and Northwest. While the north coast is well developed and dominated by the resorts of Sidári, Róda and Aharávi, the northwest remains something of a mystery to many visitors. Ágios Geórgios Págon and Ágios Stéfanos Gýrou are very different from namesake resorts south and east, respectively. The jewel of the northwest is Paleokastrítsa, boasting one of the most beautiful bays in all of Europe and retaining some charm despite its huge popularity.

The West. Between Érmones and Ágios Górdis, the west coast has superb sandy beaches. Despite often-tricky road access, they are no longer secret, and mostly well developed.

KÉRKYRA TOWN

Kérkyra Town ❶ (Corfu Town) is a beguiling place, with a relaxed, old-world elegance that rivals other Mediterranean cities many times its size. Its predominantly Venetian architecture is harmoniously flavoured with French and Georgian-English building styles, reflecting the influence of several centuries of foreign occupation. A cosmopolitan nature prevails, especially at night, when Corfiots and visitors stroll along the Listón and rendezvous at the many cafés and restaurants. In early August the atmosphere is very Italian.

⊙ ARRIVING IN THE CAPITAL

If you are driving into Kérkyra Town, it's best to park just south of the Old Town, in the vicinity of the Archaeological Museum, especially along Dimokratías Avenue, where street parking is free. Parking at the old harbour, or along the Spianáda, tempting as that might seem, is heavily controlled and expensive. Driving in Kérkyra Town is less stressful than its myriad streets would suggest, thanks to an efficient one-way system.

Public buses set down either at San Rocco Square (blue urban buses) or near the New Fort (green long-distance buses). San Rocco Square (Sarókko in Greek) can be intimidatingly busy at most times of the day. Although it is only a stone's throw away from the tourist centre of Corfu, this is a very 'Greek' part of town, with most shops and businesses – especially along Georgíou Theotóki leading up to the Puorta Reale entrance to the Old Town – catering to locals. Visitors who arrive by coach excursion disembark close to the Old Fort and the grassy gardens of the Spianáda. Those arriving by ferry at the new harbour will find it a good 1.5km (just under 1 mile) walk into town (occasional buses). For airport details see page 115.

Our description of the town inevitably involves some backtracking and close reading of the back-flap map. Kérkyra Town might be a relatively small place, but it is impossible to do justice in a single day. Try to come here on Tuesday, Thursday or Friday, when shops open in the evening.

AROUND THE SPIANÁDA (ESPLANADE)

The focal point of Kérkyra Town is the **Spianáda** (Esplanade) **Ⓐ**. Families promenade, marching bands parade and festive occasions are frequently celebrated on this broad green expanse separating the Old Fort from the rest of town. Buildings formerly here were razed in Venetian times to give a clear field of fire against enemy assault, and it was also used for fairs and jousting tournaments. The French later planted the trees and flower gardens.

On the southern half of the Spianáda is the plain **Ionian Monument**, which celebrates the island's union with Greece in 1864. It is surrounded by marble reliefs displaying the symbols

Ⓞ THAT'S CRICKET

Kérkyra Town cricket pitch is one of the most unusual sports grounds in the world. Kim Hughes, the Australian captain during the early 1980s, once hit a mighty six right over the gardens and into the moat of the Old Fort here.

The mixed cultural heritage of the island can be heard in the cricketing language. *'Play'* is the Corfiot name for cricket. But, perhaps because of the long association with the Venetians, more than one term used during play has been lifted from Italian. So when a 'long hop' becomes *primo salto* and cricket stumps are *xýla* ('woods' in Greek), the English might feel at a loss in their own game. Still, when the former England captain David Gower was asked where he had enjoyed playing the most, his immediate reply was: 'It has to be Corfu'.

Today the cricket pitch in Kérkyra Town is mainly used by the island's under-18 and under-14 youth teams, since the size of the pitch was reduced to make room for a car park. Adult matches take place in a newer, purpose-built cricket ground at Gouviá.

Palace of St Michael and St George

of the seven Ionian Islands, known as the Eptánisa in Greek. Nearby are the Victorian bandstand (where Sunday concerts are held in summer) and the Maitland Rotunda, dedicated to the first British high commissioner. At the far south end is the statue of Greece's first president (1827–31) and Corfu's greatest son, Ioannis Kapodistrias.

The Esplanade's most famous landmark is the now somewhat abbreviated cricket pitch dominating its northern half. Corfu adopted this sport during British rule, and enthusiastic local teams keep the tradition alive with matches during the season.

Across the north side of the Spianáda stands the imposing **Palace of St Michael and St George Ⓑ**, erected between 1819 and 1824 by Maltese masons as the residence for the British high commissioners, with a neoclassical façade of 32 Doric columns linking triumphal arches. It also housed the Ionian senate. When the British left, Greek royalty used it as a summer residence. The

Spianada, Kérkyra Town

bronze toga-clad figure that stands above a lily pond in front of the palace is Sir Frederick Adam, Britain's second high commissioner. The pool and its water-spouts are there to remind people that Adam was the first to ensure Kérkyra Town a reliable water supply, with an aqueduct system still in use today.

The palace's staterooms now house the **Museum of Asian Art** (www.matk.gr; Apr–Oct daily 8am–8pm, Nov–Mar 8.30am–4pm). Its collection of nearly 11,000 Asian artefacts, amassed by two Greek diplomats, is one of the most comprehensive of its kind in the world. Pieces in the east wing include funerary statuary and bowls, carved wood, pottery and blue-and-white porcelain from various Chinese dynasties. The west wing features a superb miscellany donated in 1974: Hindu and Jain deities, erotic scenes, Gandhara relief work, and Buddhist devotional art from every south Asian nation. Since 2015 there has been a permanent exhibition of Japanese folding screens and painted hanging scrolls, as well as woodblock prints by such masters as Hokusai and Utamaro. Other displays document the Noh and Kyogen theatre, plus the armour and weaponry of a Samurai warrior.

Around the back of the palace (on the Old Fort side), facing lovely sea-view gardens, is the lesser-known **Municipal Art Gallery** (http://artcorfu.gr; Tue–Sun 10am–4pm), a modest, eight-room collection comprising mostly 19th and 20th century works by

Corfiot artists. Look for the *Assassination of Kapodistrias* in Room 2 – portraying the murder of the island's most famous native son – as well as George Samartzis' charming, French-inspired *Night in Corfu* in Room 5, which shows that even in 1913, the Listón was the place to be.

The elegant arcades of the **Listón** Ⓒ border the west side of the Spianáda. Modelled on the Rue de Rivoli in Paris, it was erected by the French in 1807. Its name comes from the 'list' of noble families who were the only ones initially permitted to walk here. These days everyone gathers at the many cafés and bars under the arches or beneath the trees along the green. During the evening pedestrianised Eleftherías out front is transformed into a bustling promenade of Corfiots and visitors alike, from dapper elderly men to smartly dressed families.

Stroll down the length of **Kapodistríou Street**, which runs from behind the Listón to the southern end of the green. It is lined with handsome townhouses, most of which were built by the Venetian-era aristocracy, and several picturesque perpendicular streets lead off into town. Moustoxýdou Street, for example, used to be an important thoroughfare and was also the setting for jousting displays during Carnival, with the judges seated on the balcony above the ornate portico of the Ricchi mansion. At the very end of Kapodistríou, on Ioníou Akadimías, looms the pink façade of the former Ionian Academy, founded in 1824 by Lord Guilford as the first modern Greek university. Like much of the surrounding area, it has been completely rebuilt after suffering destruction in the heavy bombing of 1943, and today appropriately is used by the University of the Ionian.

Dousmáni Street cuts across the Esplanade to the Old Fort. Here you will find a string of colourful 19th-century horse-cabs (*carrozzi*), which will take you on a ride around Kérkyra Town. Be sure to agree on the fare before you set out.

Entry to the Old Fort over the Contrafossa bridge

THE PALEÓ FROÚRIO (OLD FORT)

Kérkyra Town grew up on the eastern peninsula around the **Paleó Froúrio** ⓓ (Old Fort; Apr–Oct daily 8am–8pm, Nov–Mar 8.30am–3pm), first established by the Byzantines during the 6th century after the Ostrogoth raids. The two peaks of the promontory on which it stands were the source of the name Corfu, a corruption of *koryfí* (summit in Greek).

A statue of Count Johann Matthias von der Schulenburg, the German mercenary who led the Corfiot defence against the Turkish attack of 1716, stands outside the fortress's west gate, one of the many fortifications added by the Venetians to the older Byzantine citadel on the eastern peak. Its defensive moat, the Contrafossa, is lined with small fishing boats and utility sheds, making for a very picturesque and peaceful scene. In turbulent times in the past, the bridge beyond the gate could be raised, cutting off land access to the fort.

The Venetian administration was based here; subsequently the British built barracks and a military hospital. The fort was then used by the Greek army until 1979. Immediately to the right upon entering, inside the former Venetian chapel, awaits an excellent collection of Byzantine mosaics and icons rescued from chapels and villas across Corfu. Further along, a path to the right leads to the neoclassical garrison church of **Ágios Geórgios**, built by the British in 1840 as an Anglican chapel and restored after damage during World War II. Now converted to a Greek Orthodox church, it has a fine stone iconostasis and icons but, thanks partly to its origins, is plain and box-like inside; interior columns disappeared during the restoration.

Come back toward the entrance, where a stone path leads past a Venetian clocktower up to the lighthouse on the higher peak. The steep climb is well worth it for the spectacular panorama of Kérkyra Town (best in the morning), Mandráki yacht harbour, the mainland coast and Mt Pandokrátor to the north.

FROM THE LISTÓN TO THE NÉO FROÚRIO

From the northern end of the Listón, walk along Kapodistríou Street, past the Corfu Reading Society (not open to the general public), and enter Arseníou Street. Look back to your right for a fine view of the Old Fort and its marina. Immediately below you is the small promontory of **Faliráki ❺**, with a couple of café-bars and a swimming lido.

Combined ticket

You can save a considerable amount on site admissions by buying a combined ticket for €14 (€7 Nov–Mar). This allows entry to the Mon Repos villa at Paleópolis, the Museum of Asian Art, the Andivouniótissa Byzantine Museum and the Old Fort, over a period of three days.

The densely wooded islet just offshore is **Vídos**, today a nature reserve but once a base for the Ottoman attacks of 1537 and 1716. More famously, the island served as a quarantine station for the most hopeless cases of the 150,000-strong Serbian army who retreated to Corfu in early 1916. About 1,200 casualties were buried on the island itself (they are now commemorated by a mausoleum), but the burial capacity of rocky Vídos was soon exceeded, and almost 10,000 more were buried at sea adjacent, an episode immortalised in the poem by Serb Milutin Bojić, *Plava Grobica* (Blue Grave – also with a memorial plaque on Vídos). Today, boats regularly shuttle in season between the island and Corfu's old port; on Vídos there are two beaches and a taverna as well as the Serbian memorials.

A short way along Arseníou Street, a flight of steps leads to the excellent **Mousío Andivouniótissas** (Byzantine Museum) **F**, housed in the eponymous 15th-century basilica (www.antivouniotissamuseum.gr; Tue–Sun 8am–3pm). The single-aisle, timber-roofed church is one of the oldest and richest on the island, with an *exonarthex* (vestibule) surrounding it on three sides. This is used today to exhibit an impressive array of icons from the 15th to 19th centuries, many of the so-called 'Cretan School'; after the fall of Crete to the Ottomans, many highly skilled artists came as refugees to Venetian-held Corfu. Standouts include two icons by 16th-century master Mihaïl Damaskinos, and a dramatic *Mē mou haptou* from the next century by Emmanouil Tzanes.

Around the corner, the imposing profile of the **Néo Froúrio** (New Fort) **G** (daily 9am–3.30pm, 8am–8pm in summer) heaves into view beyond the old port. The New Fort was built by the Venetians between 1572 and 1645, shortly after the first major Ottoman siege. You can see the Venetian emblem – the winged lion of St Mark – in stone relief above the massive gates. The French, and later the British, elaborated the

The New Fort

fortifications. The town's fruit and vegetable market is now held in the dry moat on the western side. A series of secret tunnels is said to connect the new and old fortresses (and even Vídos). Occasionally, temporary exhibitions or concerts are held inside the walls, but the finest sight is the superb late-afternoon view of Kérkyra Town and the mainland coast.

THE COMMERCIAL CENTRE

The town centre essentially lies between the New Fort and the Esplanade, a warren of narrow, pedestrianised, marble-paved lanes arranged in discrete, historic districts. The main commercial artery, linking the Listón and the old harbour in Spiliá district, is **Nikifórou Theotóki** – just one of several thoroughfares named after members of this long-established, illustrious Corfiot family. To the south, in Pórta Remoúnda district, and north, in the Kofinéta neighbourhood, numerous parallel streets intersect Kapodistríou.

The main square along Nikifórou Theotóki is officially **Platía Iróön Kypriakón Agonistón** (Square of the Cypriot Fighters), with a statue of Corfiot politician Georgios Theotoki (1843–1916) in the middle; however, because the west side of the plaza is bounded by the 1846-vintage building that once housed the island's oldest bank, the Ioniki (Ionian), everybody calls it **Platía Ionikí**. Four galleries on the upper storey above the present-day Alpha Bank here are home to the **Banknote Museum** ⊕ (www.

⊙ ST SPYRIDON

Corfiots pray to him, swear by him, name their sons after him and honour him with a remarkable passion. He is the island's beloved patron saint, yet he wasn't even born on Corfu. Spyridon was a village shepherd on the distant island of Cyprus. He became a monk, then a bishop, and was noted for his devoutness and ability to effect minor miracles. After his death in AD 348, a sweet odour wafted from his grave; his body was exhumed and found to be perfectly preserved. The saint's remains were taken to Constantinople, but were smuggled out (with those of St Theodora Augusta) before the Turkish occupation in 1453. Unceremoniously wrapped in a sack of straw strapped to a mule, the remains arrived in Corfu in 1456. In time, Spyridon became the object of enthusiastic veneration.

To honour his miracles, his casket is paraded colourfully through Kérkyra Town on Orthodox Palm Sunday, Easter Saturday, 11 August, and the first Sunday in November. St Spyridon has reputedly saved the island four times: twice from the plague, once from famine, and once (in 1716) from the Turks. Small wonder that numerous Corfiot men are named Spyros (the diminutive of Spyridon).

alphapolitismos.gr/gr/05-Banknote-Museum; Apr–Sep Wed–Fri 9am–2pm, Wed and Fri 5–8.30pm, Sat–Sun 8.30am–3pm, winter Wed–Sun 8am–3pm), featuring an extensive display of every Greek drachma (the pre-euro currency) denomination issued as well as Ionian Bank shares and documents. Much more interesting than it sounds, this impressive collection illustrates all the stages in designing, printing and releasing notes for circulation.

The bell tower of Ágios Spyrídon

Across from the bank stands **Faneroméni** church, also called **Panagía ton Xénon** (Our Lady of the Foreigners) because it was used by refugees from the mainland during the Ottoman occupation. Erected in 1689, it is lavishly decorated with gilded wood, a beautifully painted ceiling and icons by Cretan painters. Opposite is a simpler church, **Ágios Ioánnis o Pródromos** (St John the Baptist). Built in 1520, it was formerly Corfu's cathedral and also contains important Cretan-school icons.

The red-domed bell tower of the church of **Ágios Spyrídon ❶**, the tallest on the island, rises north of the square, at the top of the broad stairway known as the Plakáda t'Agíou. It was founded in 1590 to house the mummified body of Corfu's beloved patron saint, who lies in an ornate silver coffin in a shrine to the right of the altar. On certain days the casket is opened, and on special feast days the saint is paraded upright

The marble-clad Town Hall

through the town. His shrunken face can be seen through a glass panel, and his slippered feet are exposed for the faithful to kiss. With all the opulent Venetian oil lamps swinging above the casket (plus the chandeliers and the candelabra), this modest, dimly lit church is said to have the greatest amount of silver of any Greek church outside the island of Tínos. Frescoes on the ceiling depict the saint's miracles.

Leave the church by the door onto Agíou Spyrídonos Street, turning left to meet Filarmonikís Street. Here you can turn right to explore the Campiello district (see page 42). Alternatively you can turn left to reach M. Theotóki Street to see more of the shopping district. (If you have time do both, see the Old Town first and then retrace your steps.)

Follow M. Theotóki Street south, past the lovely, compact **Platía Vrahlióti** with a well in the centre, until emerging onto tiered **Platía Dimarhíou** ❶ (Town Hall Square), offically Platía Mihaïl Theotóki.

At the bottom end sits the **Dimarhío (Town Hall)**, one of Corfu's most decorative buildings. Built by the Venetians in 1665 out of white marble from the eastern slopes of Mt Pandokrátor, its original single-storey loggia served as a meeting place for the nobility. It was converted into the San Giacomo Theatre in 1720, and later a second storey was added. It became the Town Hall in 1903 when the municipal theatre (destroyed in 1943) was constructed. The façade is adorned with carved masks and medallions. On the eastern wall there is a bust of Francesco Morosini, the Venetian commander who defeated the Ottomans at Athens in 1687.

The tiers of the plaza are crowded with the tables of a popular café and expensive, touristy restaurants; in off hours local boys find the layout irresistible for skateboarding. The imposing building diagonally opposite the Dimarhío is the **Catholic Cathedral of Ágii Iákovos ke Hristóforos** (SS James and Christopher), dating from 1632. It is frequently open for use by Corfu's large Catholic community, about 3,000 strong and entirely descended from 19th-century Maltese stonemasons brought here by the British.

From Platía Dimarhíou, continue south into the lanes of Pórta Remoúnda, where the main sight, at Moustoxýdou 19, is the **Serbian Museum ⓚ** (Mon–Fri 9am–2pm), which with military paraphernalia, documents and photographs meticulously documents the experiences of the Serbian army and government-in-exile here during World War I, when over 150,000 soldiers rested at scattered campsites between Pyrgí and Moraïtika from January 1916 onwards. Besides Greece, the only one of their notional allies who provided supplies or medical assistance to the defeated army in an official capacity was France – though a period poster, issued by a US-based relief committee, makes interesting reading ('Save Serbia, Our Ally') in light of the American 1990s demonisation of the country. The refugees got on famously with their hosts – there were no reports of looting or other improper behaviour – and a number of marriages with local girls resulted, as about 10,000 Serbs stayed on Corfu until 1918.

THE OLD TOWN

The **Old Town** is the fascinating maze of narrow streets, steep stairways and arched alleys squeezed into the northern half of Kérkyra Town, between the Spianáda and the old port. It has been described as Greece's largest 'living medieval town'. As you wander along the marble-paved streets, you might feel that this traffic-free quarter of tottering multi-storey buildings is like a miniature Venice – minus the canals, of course; the northernmost part has even retained its Venetian name, **Campiello** . There are many ways of entering the Campiello, and it is an excellent place to simply wander at will.

In Venetian times, the area between the old and new forts was surrounded by city walls (demolished during the 19th century). As Corfiots weren't permitted to live outside the fortifications, the only direction in which they could expand their dwellings was upwards, producing the district's unusually high architecture. And, just as in the less-touristy parts of Venice, much of the district's appeal is in its residential atmosphere, with laundry strung across alleyways, old women sitting on stools weaving or keeping an eye on babies, and cats snoozing in tiny sun-splashed squares. The only 'sight' is the charming 17th-century **Venetian Well** on the Campiello's Platía Kremastí (officially Líla Desýlla), where a notable restaurant sets out its tables.

From just below Platía Kremastí, Agías Theodóras Street leads to Corfu's **Orthodox Cathedral** , built in 1577 and dedicated to St Theodora Augusta, the island's second-most-revered saint (after Spyridon). Her headless body, which was spirited out of Constantinople (along with Spyridon's), lies in

Tomb of the Menecrates

a silver reliquary to the right of the altar screen. Broad flights of steps lead down to the old harbour, and Corfiots used to momentarily pause here to light a candle before or after a sea journey (less so now that ferries use the new port).

From just below the cathedral, traverse restaurant-and-café-rich Spiliá district along Prosaléndou, then Solomoú, streets, watching for signs indicating Corfu's sole surviving synagogue in the old Evraïkí (Jewish) quarter. The **Scuola Greca** (May–Sept Mon–Sat 10am–3pm) at Velissaríou 4 has been lovingly restored, and the upstairs prayer hall has a memorial plaque to the nearly 2,000 local Jews deported to Auschwitz in June 1944 (about 150 survived). The local community of about 60 can no longer support a rabbi; one comes from Israel for the major holidays.

The sojourn of the Durrell family on Corfu continues to exert a strong grip on the British imagination, helped along by the

2016–19 ITV series. Opposite the Scuola Greca, at Velissaríou 7, **The Durrell Spot** is a small shop peddling books by and about Gerald and Lawrence. Assorted Durrellian experiences can also be arranged here.

Also nearby, the **Sapounopoïïa Patouni/Patounis Soap Factory ⓞ**, on Platía Saróko at Ioánnou Theotóki 9 (www.patounis.gr; Mon–Sat 9.30am–2pm, also Tue, Thu and Fri 6–8.30pm), is the last remaining olive-oil soap factory on Corfu, operating here since 1891. The cool, fragrant premises (a listed monument) are themselves a highlight. Free English-language tours (Mon–Fri at noon) permit a glimpse of the soap being logo-stamped in its moulds, then cut into bars. Do buy one or two (great gifts!) upon leaving; 'green laundry soap' removes just about any grease stain from clothing.

ARCHAEOLOGICAL TREASURES

From the Scuola Greca, the Patounis Factory or the Serbian Museum it's a short, pleasant walk south – along the coastal avenue in the latter case – to the island's **Archaeological Museum ⓟ** (Wed–Mon 8.30am–3pm).

This renovated two-storey building houses superb artefacts from all periods of ancient Korkyra, starting on the ground floor with dioramas and a few Mesolithic items, plus a small, later bronze statuette of Herakles by the entry. The star attraction upstairs, the **Gorgon pediment** (c.580 BC) comes from the Temple of Artemis and is so named for central, sculpted Gorgó (one of three snake-haired sister-gorgons), shown 3m/10ft tall with wings at her shoulders, winged sandals, and serpents at her waist. She is flanked by her offspring, born from her dying blood: Pegasus, the winged horse, and the hero Khrysaor. Beside her two alert lion-panthers wait to obey the commands of this monster who, according to myth, turned anyone who met her gaze to

Sculpture of Maria in a British cemetery

stone. The pediment was discovered in 1912 at Paleópolis and is Greece's oldest existing monumental sculpture.

Not so colossal – but almost as important archaeologically – is the Archaic Lion of Menekrates. This late 7th-century BC sculpture, in near-perfect condition, was found in 1843 and is thought to have graced the grave of a warrior during Korkyra's struggle for independence from Corinth. It is considered one of the most beautiful ancient animal sculptures.

Among the museum's other treasures, unjustly eclipsed by the Gorgon pediment, are poignant child-grave offerings (toy rabbits, sheep, plus feeding bottles) and a small pediment from 500 BC, showing the god Dionysos and a youth reclining at a symposium, holding a *rhyton* (pouring vessel) and a *kylix* (drinking cup) respectively. A dozen small statues of the goddess Artemis in her avatar as mistress of beasts are thought to have been produced as votive offerings for local worshippers.

Some three blocks southwest of the museum stands the **tomb of Menekrates**, on Maraslí, a circular structure with a conical roof honouring a mercenary who fought for Korkyra. It dates from about 600 BC. Continue inland along this street, then west onto Kolokotróni, to the serenely beautiful **British Cemetery ❼**. Among the tall cypress trees and meticulously kept flowers and shrubbery (beautiful wild flowers, even orchids, also grow here) lie graves dating from 1814 to recent years of civilian and of British servicemen from the two World Wars. The circular wall south of the cemetery encloses the local, British-built **jail** (*fylakí*). This was once the most modern penal institute in Europe, with individual cells for inmates. It is still in use today, though ironically having one of the worst reputations in Greece.

SOUTHERN SUBURBS

To explore this part of Corfu you will need transport, or be willing to hop on and off blue city buses marked '2 KANONI'. Head south along the coastal road for about 2km (a mile or so) and turn inland (right) to the Byzantine **Church of Ágii Iáson ke Sosípatros ❽** (daily 8.30am–2pm), one of only two Byzantine churches surviving intact on the island. It is dedicated to saints Jason and Sosipater, the evangelists credited with bringing Christianity to Corfu in the 2nd century. The present church dates back to about 1000, and conforms to a type then popular on the Greek

Kardáki Spring

Near the roundabout at Análipsi, a steep path leads down to Kardáki Spring. The water that flows from the mouth of a stone lion – cool in the summer and warm in the winter – is reputed never to dry up. Legend has it that anyone who drinks from the spring is destined to return to Corfu.

Vlacherna Monastery

mainland – a domed, cross-in-square ground plan with a narthex and triple apse. The black marble columns separating the narthex from the main church, and huge poros blocks in the walls, come from ancient buildings. Few frescoes have survived, but there are fine icons in the Baroque chancel.

Further along the road to Kanóni stands the entrance to the villa and gardens of **Mon Repos** ⑤. Built in 1820 by High Commissioner Frederick Adam as a summer residence, it later became the property of the Greek royal family. Prince Philip, the Duke of Edinburgh, was born here in 1921. Mon Repos was subsequently the subject of an ownership dispute between ex-king Constantine and the government, only resolved in 1996. Since then the villa has been restored and now contains the Museum of Paleópolis (late Apr–late Oct Thu–Tue 8.30am–4pm, winter closes 3pm). While the contents are not generally world beating, the displays are well laid out and labelled, with interesting

Corfu's most popular tourist sight: the Achilleion Palace

temporary exhibits. There are period furnishings from Adams' time, a useful interactive model of the ancient town and environs, photos of archaeological digs, and a wealth of thematically arranged finds from the grounds of the estate, especially the shrine at Kardáki. Paths outside wind along the wooded promontory, past a derelict chapel, to a scenic viewpoint; from here it's another 15 minutes' walk to the remains of a small Doric temple dating from 500 BC.

Ancient Korkyra

Opposite the Mon Repos gate lie the commanding ruins of the originally 5th-century **basilica of Iovianós** 🚇 (Agía Kérkyra; open irregularly), oldest church on the island, constructed from remnants of nearby pagan temples. Once five-aisled, it was ruined by invaders, rebuilt to a smaller scale during ensuing centuries, then destroyed again in World War II before being partially restored in 2000.

The original Corinthian-founded city of Korkyra sprawled over much of the area between Mon Repos and Kanóni, now called **Paleópolis**. A narrow road behind the Roman baths (open) opposite the basilica leads to the hamlet of Análipsi, thought to be the location of the ancient acropolis, unsurprisingly with excellent views over Mon Repos.

Along the road toward Kanóni, you'll see a side road marked 'Stratía'. Here are the ruins of the **Temple of Artemis**, source of the Gorgon Pediment. Next door is the well-kept monastery of **Agíon Theodóron**. At the end of this road stands the only surviving section of the ancient city wall, a 5th-century BC tower, which in Byzantine times became the church of **Panagía Neratzíha**.

Kanóni

Generations of earlier visitors knew **Kanóni ❷** as a tranquil green peninsula, a pleasant walk or carriage ride south of the capital. Popular with Corfiots, it also attracted large groups of British residents, who came to admire the most famous view on the island: the two islets resting peacefully just outside the Halikopoúlou lagoon.

Times have changed, as modern hotels and blocks of flats have disfigured the landscape. The motivation for building here is unclear, as most views are of the shallow, muddy lagoon (an important bird haven and the adjacent airport runway, complete with thunderous sound effects. Kanóni's name derives from the gun battery that the French installed on the hillside here in 1798. Nevertheless, the delightful picture-postcard **view** of the islets and the coastal scenery beyond them remains intact.

The islet in the foreground – linked to the mainland by a causeway – is not Mouse Island but **Vlahérna**, which is home to a pretty, white, post-Byzantine convent (Panagía Vlahernón; usually shut). Densely vegetated **Mouse Island** (or Pondikonísi), home to a tiny Byzantine chapel, a gift shop and small café, lies a three-minute boat trip away. Mouse Island is the main contender for the site of the mythical Odyssean ship turned to stone (see page 16).

A pair of café-restaurants on the hillside provide a relaxing terrace from which to enjoy the magnificent view. A pedestrian causeway below leads across the lagoon to Pérama.

The Achilleion Palace

With a romantic past as an imperial hideaway forming a large part of its attraction, the **Achilleion (Ahíllio) Palace ❸** (Apr–Oct Mon–Sat 8am–7pm, Sun 8am–2.30pm; Nov–Mar 9am–3.30pm) is one of the most popular sights on the island, and usually teeming with tour groups. Used as a location in the James Bond film *For Your Eyes Only*, the palace is situated some 10km (6 miles) south of Kérkyra Town.

The beautiful Empress Elisabeth of Austria (nicknamed Sisi) fell in love with this site on a visit to the island during the 1860s. In 1889 – desperately unhappy in her marriage, stifled by the pomp of Vienna and devastated by the suicide of her only son – she bought this land and commissioned the building of a palace that would be worthy of her idol, the Greek hero Achilles. The result, built in extreme neoclassical style, was immediately criticised as being tasteless and ostentatious. It was described by British writer Lawrence Durrell as 'a monstrous building' and by the American Henry Miller as 'the worst piece of gimcrackery I have ever laid eyes on'.

The empress nonetheless spent as much time as she possibly could at the Achilleion, in utmost seclusion in the spring and autumn of each year. But poor Sisi had only seven years to enjoy her palace. Her tragic life came to a premature end in 1898 when, during a visit to Geneva, she was mortally stabbed by an Italian anarchist.

In 1908 Kaiser Wilhelm II of Germany acquired the palace from Sisi's daughter, inviting dignitaries from

Statue highlight

Among all the statues scattered about the grounds, only one is considered by experts to have any artistic merit: the dramatic *Dying Achilles*, by German sculptor Ernst Herter.

all over Europe to attend parties and concerts here. Because most arrived by boat, he built a bridge at the seashore that crossed the coastal road to paths leading directly to his palace. Only the ruins of the bridge, ironically destroyed by the German army in autumn 1943, remain today. The Kaiser also installed an awkward 4.5-ton bronze *Victorious Achilles*, which looms some 11.5m (38ft) high at the far end of the formal gardens.

Kaiser Wilhelm's bronze Achilles

The Achilleion was used as a military hospital during World War I by the Serbs and the French (whose casualties lie in a cemetery just downhill). In 1919 it became the property of the Greek government, as war reparations, and from 1962 to 1983 its opulent upper floors were converted into a casino. In the 1990s, after renovation and the removal of its casino, the palace was opened to the public, though only half a dozen ground-floor rooms can be visited.

The Achilleion is adorned throughout by pseudo-Classical statues, with Greek gods, goddesses and heroes filling every corner. Those surrounding the Peristyle of the Muses, behind the palace, are copies of the ones in Rome's Villa Borghese gardens. Do make sure to peer through the window here to see the giant painting *The Triumph of Achilles* by Franz Matz. (It is on the first floor of the palace, which is closed to the public.) Our hero is shown in brutal, vengeful form dragging the body of Hector behind his chariot as a reprisal for the killing of Achilles' friend Patroklos.

Inside, the ground-floor rooms house a small chapel and the original furnishings and memorabilia of the empress and the Kaiser. One unusual attraction is the adjustable saddle on which Wilhelm used to sit while writing at his desk.

The extensive grounds are perhaps the true highlight of the Achilleion. The manicured formal gardens are a real pleasure, with magnificent sweeping views over the island.

THE SOUTH

Benítses ❹, some 12km (7.5 miles) south of the capital, no longer the island's nonstop party town, now attracts a much quieter clientele. The town has also revamped its image with the opening of

☉ THE VENERABLE OLIVE

Almost every Corfiot owns a few olive trees. In Venetian times, peasants received a bonus for every 100 trees planted, and by the 17th century a family's wealth was determined by the number of trees it had. Today there are perhaps 3.5 million of them on the island.

According to legend, St Spyridon appeared in an olive grove and proclaimed that cutting or beating the trees was cruel. As a result, for many years Corfiots neither pruned the branches nor picked the fruit. Instead, they let the olives fall to the ground naturally, where huge nets were spread to catch them. Today, however, pruning – and some combing out of the fruit – is practiced. Trees bear fruit only every other year and might take 12 years to yield a first crop.

a smart new marina opposite the main square.

Benítses has been settled since at least Roman times; behind the harbour square stand the meagre remains of what was once a Roman bathhouse, and local spring water is still esteemed. This old village centre, near the port, has a very Greek atmosphere, with pretty cottages that retain the character of the original fishing settlement. The lush valley at the western edge of town is crisscrossed with footpaths in an unexpected wilderness.

Sea shore taverna at Boúkari

MORAÏTIKA AND MESONGÍ

The busy coastal road continues south as far as the contiguous resorts of Moraïtika and Mesongí, 20km (12.5 miles) from Kérkyra Town. They lie at the mouth of – and are divided by – the Mesongí river (rowboat ferries cross it). This is an attractive spot, with fishing and pleasure boats moored alongside the riverfront.

Moraïtika ❺ is the busier and livelier of the pair. Its older section is set on a hill just off the main road and marked by a red-and-yellow *kambanarió* (bell tower). There is no tourist development up here, just an attractive taverna or two providing a nice contrast to the seaside resort below. Like Moraïtika, **Mesongí** ❻ features an increasing amount of development, now spreading back from the long, but very narrow beaches. Behind the beach, Mesongí has some of Corfu's oldest olive groves,

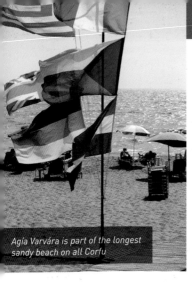

Agía Varvára is part of the longest sandy beach on all Corfu

planted by the Venetians over 500 years ago.

From here the main road south curves inland and reaches a T-junction at Áno Mesongí. The route north takes you inland through the pastoral scenery of the Mesongí river valley before ascending the slopes of Corfu's second-tallest mountain, the 576m (1,889ft) Ágii Déka ('Ten Saints'). From **Ágii Déka village ⑦** there are spectacular views over Benítses and the distant Kanóni Peninsula.

An alternative route to the southern tip of the island involves following the minor road that runs along the coast southeast from Mesongí. Along this peaceful, tree-shaded shore are small seafood tavernas and narrow, pebbly beaches where you can soak up the tranquil bay view. This pretty stretch ends at the small fishing village of **Boúkari**. But if you would like a little more of the same, you can continue along the coast road to Petrití, a modern annexe of more attractive **Korakádes**, just uphill.

SOUTHWEST BEACHES

Directly opposite here, on Corfu's southwest coast, lies the island's longest sandy beach, divided into various resorts. To reach it from Boúkari, return to the main road where the old monastery at Argyrádes sports a striking Venetian belfry. Head east for 2km (1.2 miles) and at Marathiás village a sign to **Paralía**

Marathiá points to the right, down to the beach; the road forks, with the left option skirting a small stream separating the contiguous stretch of beach known as **Agía Varvára** ❽. It's easy enough to ford the stream on foot, but by car the low-key development at Agía Varvára is accessible only by a separate road from Perivóli village. Together they form an attractive broad stretch of soft golden sand, with a few naturists under the cliffs of the Agía Varvára section.

The turning for the much busier resort of **Ágios Geórgios Argyrádon** heads down just west of Argyrádes. Development sprawls for about 2km (a mile or so) along the frontage road, but the beach is as good as Agía Varvára or Marathiá, made of the same golden sand. The resort strip ends at bit further west at **Íssos** ❾, which borders the lagoon of Korission. Drivers are better off returning to the main road, head west and then descending at the signposted turning. The scenery at Íssos is quite wild, with high dunes providing shelter for nudists, and large wind-carved rock outcrops. This was a setting for a chase scene in the James Bond film *For Your Eyes Only*. Windsurfing conditions are excellent, though the school has closed down.

On the far side of the channel that feeds the brackish lagoon is **Halikoúnas** beach, perhaps not quite as spectacular as Íssos but with separate kitesurfing and windsurfing schools, pockets of naturism, beach bars and a better selection of full-service tavernas at the far end. Road access is via

The Korissíon Lagoon

This lagoon was artificially created with a channel from the sea by the Venetians as a fish nursery, for which it is still used. Today it is a protected area, off-limits for swimming or boating, but bird-watchers will find plenty to observe here, in spring or autumn.

Áno Mesongí, past a memorial to the Serbian Drina Division and the octagonal Byzantine **castle of Gardíki** ⑩ (always open) with recently restored ramparts and gatehouse, although with little visible inside.

KÁVOS

Southeast of Marathiás sprawls a fertile landscape devoted to fruit orchards, market gardens, yet more olive groves and Corfu's principal wine-producing region. **Lefkímmi** is the hub of this primarily agricultural region, bypassed by a very fast road that goes all the way to the southern tip of the island. **Kávos** ⑪ is the end of the road, the last resort – in just about every respect. To Corfiots and foreigners alike, the name is synonymous with young booze-fuelled revellers, clubbing and partying. But lately its abundant accommodation and dozen music clubs work to half-capacity at best, even in July and August. That said, the soft sandy beach that extends for 3km (nearly 2 miles) shelves gently and is popular with families earlier in the season. Boat excursions, however, leave from Lefkímmi's port.

Just over 3km south lies Cape Asprókavos, Corfu's southernmost tip, and the ruined but atmospheric, well-signposted **Panagía Arkoudílas monastery**, overlooking superb Kánoula beach.

NORTH OF KÉRKYRA TOWN

The former fishing villages northwest of Kérkyra Town are now home to some of the island's liveliest and most popular resorts. Kondókali and Gouviá lie within a sheltered lagoon about 8km (5 miles) from the capital. They are set back from the busy main highway and linked by a small road, with side tracks leading to sand and pebble beaches and a large marina.

Gouviá ⑫ is the more developed of the two, with a narrow, compacted sand beach dominated by large hotels. One section is even fronted with concrete so that the sea (shallow and still at this point) looks more like a municipal boating pond than the Ionian. The sheltered bay is largely taken up by an extensive yacht marina – appropriately enough, as it was once a Venetian naval base and the skeletal arches of an old Venetian *arsenáli* (boatyard) survive at the end of Gouviá's beach.

Across the pretty bay the little church of **Ypapandí** (Candlemas; Presentation of Christ), juts out on a stone spit rather like the famous 'Mouse Island'. Beyond the confines of the lagoon is **Lazarétto** ⑬ island, with a grim history – the Venetians established a leprosarium on it, the World War II occupying powers confined (and shot) members of the Greek resistance here, and after the Greek civil war it served as a place for executing condemned communists.

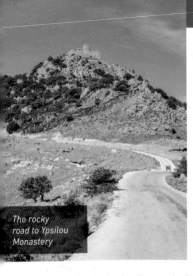

The rocky road to Ypsilou Monastery

The resort of **Dasiá** features dense olive groves between the main road and the sea, but otherwise consists merely of a long string of restaurants, shops and bars along a very busy main road. A long, narrow and often crowded beach is tucked away down side roads, with various water-sports on offer. The continual stream of colourful parasails against the blue sky – with olive groves and mountains in the background – is a fine sight.

To escape the hustle and bustle, wander inland on an uphill journey past quiet villas and olive groves to **Káto Korakiána ⑭**. Here, installed in an old, three-storey Venetian villa, is the **National Gallery Annexe of Corfu** (Wed, Thu, Sat and Sun 8.30am–3.30pm; Fri 10am–2pm and 6–9pm; http://corfu.nation algallery.gr/en/parartema-kerkyras-plerophories). There are 150 works of prominent Greek painters from all eras since 1830, on permanent loan from the Athens parent collection.

The contiguous resorts of **Ýpsos** and **Pyrgí ⑮** flank a wide, beautiful bay about 15km (9.5 miles) north of Kérkyra Town. They are trying to re-invent themselves as family havens after many years of patronage by armies of young, largely British singles. The long, narrow beach lining the bay is a mixture of sand and shingle.

In times past, Ýpsos Bay was a target for pirates and Ottoman raiders; supposedly the name *Ýpsos* ('heights') was a ruse to dissuade them from mounting an attack. *Pyrgí*, meaning 'tower', probably derives from a watchtower built to warn of imminent raids. The resorts themselves are recent creations, developing around resettlements of villagers from Ágios Márkos whose homes were destroyed by landslides in the 1950s. Ýpsos at least has retained its fishing fleet, tucked away in an attractive little harbour behind the road as you enter from the south.

MT PANDOKRÁTOR

Just beyond Pyrgí, a road leads – via Strinýlas – to the top of **Mt Pandokrátor** (911m/2,989ft). Beyond a series of corkscrew bends you'll be greeted by stupendous views over Ýpsos Bay. Just below the colourful village of Spartýlas, the road broadens out into a rolling landscape of fruit trees, fields and vineyards where some of Corfu's finest wine is produced. Between Strinýlas and Petália, signs indicate the final approach to Mt Pandokrátor.

This side road is emphatically not to be driven in bad weather, and parking space at the summit is limited – best to leave cars below the final zigzag and walk up the last hundred metres. On a clear day you will be rewarded with unbeatable views: the entire sickle outline of Corfu and, over the narrow channel, a glimpse of Albania. To the south, in the blue Ionian Sea, lie the islands of Paxí and distant Lefkáda. Sadly, closer up the view now includes the aftermath of an August 2011 forest fire that devastated much of Mt Pandokrátor.

Making the ascent

It is also possible to get to the top of Mt Pandokrátor from the northeastern part of the island (see page 65). A good tour choice is to go up one side and come down the other.

Barbati Beach

The summit monastery of **Ypsiloú Pandokrátora** 🔟 (Apr–Oct 7am–12.30pm and 2.30–8pm), which shares space with an ugly, 86m (282ft) antenna erected by the 1967–74 military junta to beam propaganda into Albania, was constructed during the 17th century on the site of a 1347 vintage church that had been built by nearby villagers. Restored in recent years, it is a dark, peaceful haven with many frescoes and an ornate *témblon* (icon screen), but just one monk.

THE NORTHEAST

The dramatic beauty of northeastern Corfu begins above Ýpsos Bay and ends near Kassiópi, a lovely drive over a winding, narrow but paved road covering some 20km (12.5 miles). The road climbs sharply into the steep green slopes that overawe the coast, offering tantalising glimpses of the sea below. There are several viewing points along this cliff-side road, but most of the shore is hidden and often accessible only by narrow, steep tracks that plunge alarmingly. Some beaches can be reached only on foot. The best way to explore is by boat, which can be arranged from most jetties – self-skippering boat-hire is very popular here. It is worth noting that all the beaches from Ýpsos to Kassiópi are pebbly. Nonetheless, swimming is excellent at nearly all the beaches along this coast.

The shift from the mass-market resorts south of Ýpsos Bay to the small and relatively less-developed coves of the northeast peninsula comes at **Barbáti ⓱**. There is no steep track to negotiate here, just a gentle slope leading down to sea level, where olive groves shelter a long, pebbly and popular beach with all the usual water sports. The mountains rise steeply behind the beach, making an attractive backdrop. There is some music from beachside and roadside bars, but the atmosphere of Barbáti is very different from that of its southern neighbours.

☉ A GLIMPSE OF ALBANIA

All along its northeast coast, Corfu looks across at the mainland of Albania. At its nearest point – on the stretch between Kalámi and Ágios Stéfanos – the shore of this now-welcoming, ex-communist land is less than 2 nautical miles away. Day trips are a popular, if somewhat expensive, means of taking a quick look. The boat journey from Kérkyra Town to the Albanian port of Sarandë (Ágii Saránda) takes 40–75 minutes round trip depending on the type of craft used. Outings vary from the basic crossing, guided tour of ancient Butrint and buffet lunch (from €53) to a more elaborate, overnight trip including an inland foray to the heritage town of Gjirokastër and Lëkurësi castle near Sarandë (around €100). Agencies in every resort offer these excursions, but you can also book directly through the shipping companies, Ionian Cruises, at the new port (tel: 26610 38690; www.ionian-cruises.com) or Meander Travel at the old port (tel: 26610 37546; www.meander-corfutravel. com). Albanian-run Sipa Tours (tel: 26610 56415 or 6976 650713; www.sipatours.com) arranges multiday tours across southern Albania, including hiking and river-rafting.

The next resort along is **Nisáki** ⑱, reached by a two-bend drive from the main road. The water here is a crystal-clear medley of greens and blues, though there is hardly room to spread your towel on its tiny pebble beach. It is undoubtedly a lovely spot, with tavernas, a cluster of shops and accommodation, but you will have to get here early (or late) to stake a beach claim.

Just a bit further on, **Kamináki** is a strong contender in the sweepstakes for 'Corfu's most terrifying beach descent'. There are two tavernas, a small watersports facility and around 100m (330ft) of attractive white-pebble beach. The next beach along, **Krouzerí**, is dominated by a huge, unsightly hotel. You will have to share the pebbles with hotel guests, but the beach is of reasonable size and there are water sports facilities plus tavernas.

Just beyond, at a tight hairpin turn, are signs pointing down to secluded **Agní** ⑲. Parking at the road's end is limited, so in peak season it's best to arrive at Agní by boat from Nisáki or Kalámi. Agní is known to lots of happy diners, many of whom come here year after year to the three tavernas overlooking the picturesque beach.

Lawrence Durrell's beloved 'White House' (https://thewhite house.gr) still stands at the far end of **Kalámi** ⑳ bay, where you can enjoy the marvellous scenery that inspired him to write *Prospero's Cell* (a hugely evocative read that describes Corfu in the days before tourism) between 1936 and 1939. Despite various vacation villas and an insensitive new hotel complex that defaces one side of the hills enclosing the bay, it remains a fairly tranquil resort.

Charming **Kouloúra** ㉑, one bay north, is scarcely

Kensington-on-Sea

The northeast coast is sometimes dubbed 'Kensington-on-Sea' after the well-heeled British visitors who holiday here.

Kassiópi, a fishing village with a long history, now a thriving resort

large enough for a handful of fishing boats and a small taverna, but is one of the most picturesque and photographed corners of Corfu. A constant stream of buses, cars and motorbikes pull up at the large parking space high above on the main road to gaze down on its classic, tiny horseshoe harbour enclosed by tall cypresses. There is not a more typically Ionian view in the archipelago. Gerald Durrell, the brother of Lawrence, lived in Kouloúra and, while there, penned the amusing *My Family and Other Animals*. There's limited parking beyond the port, towards **Houhoulió** beach.

Just past Kouloúra, yet another lovely white-pebble beach, far below, beckons invitingly to drivers from the clifftop road. It belongs to **Kerasiá**, an attractive low-key resort with a handful of villas. It is reached by the turn-off to Ágios Stéfanos or, for the energetic, via a 20-minute coastal path from Kouloúra. **Ágios Stéfanos Sinión** is the most exclusive of this coast's beautiful bays. Fishing boats and yachts bob lazily in the circular harbour, ringed

Belfry at deserted Paleá Períthia

by whitewashed cottages and tavernas. From here, a minor paved road or another path leads to more exposed **Avláki** and **Sykiá** bays, the last two before Kassiópi.

Not so long ago, **Kassiópi** 🉂 was merely a quiet fishing village. These days it's a popular little resort. In fact, Kassiópi was a thriving settlement even in Roman times, visited by Cicero, Cato and Emperor Nero, among others. It is named after the god Zeus Kassios, a cult with origins in distant Syria, and the central church of **Panagía Kassopítra** (open daily all day) stands on the site of Zeus' former temple, traces of whose floor persist two levels below the current one. This used to be the foremost shrine on Corfu before the arrival of St Spyridon. The current shrine dates from after the 1537 Ottoman sack of Corfu, with more Venetian rebuilding in around 1590, specifically fine frescoes in the apse and on the south wall, uncovered during a 2015–16 restoration. Opposite the church, the Angevins built a fortress during the 13th century to shelter the locals from pirate raids; this has been consolidated with a walkway (always open) tracing the inner wall perimeter for fine views.

The town is packed with tourists during midsummer, but local fishermen still use the deeply indented harbour. Nightlife is lively, particularly on the left (west) side of the harbour, but not in-your-face. Bathing beaches lie to either side of the resort, especially at

Kalamiónas cove west of town, and at the tip of the castle headland, where Pipítos and Bataría coves are favoured.

The most spectacular portion of the coast road ends just before Kassiópi; beyond it gentler, shrub-covered foothills border a broad coastal plain blessed with an abundance of hayfields, vines and almond trees. The first attractive sandy beach along this stretch is **Ágios Spyrídon ㉓**, 7.5km (4.5 miles) northwest of Kassiópi, a small but attractive beach with fine golden sand, a taverna and great views across to Albania.

The 'ghost town' of **Paleá Períthia ㉔** (Old Períthia, sometimes Áno Períthia), set on the northern slopes of Mt Pandokrátor and accessible by a turning opposite the road to Ágios Spyrídon, provides an interesting break from the seaside. Incredibly, Períthia was once the capital of Kassiópi district. Today there are just a handful of families resident in summer, operating a few tavernas with a beautiful view of the crumbling village and the mountain overhead. Simply sitting and savouring the peace and quiet here makes a journey well worthwhile.

No natural disaster overtook Paleá Períthia; its residents simply moved to the coast in search of work during the 1960s and 1970s. Cobbled lanes between the old stone houses, slowly being done up, and churches, provide a haunting glimpse of old Corfiot life. In spring this valley is a great spot for naturalists, who can spot hundreds of butterflies, birds and wild flowers. The long-distance Corfu Trail passes through here, descending from a saddle on the flank of Mt Pandokrátor.

THE NORTH

Corfu's north shore features an 8km (5 mile) expanse of sand stretching from Cape Róda through Aharávi and beyond to Cape Agía Ekateríni. Although the width of the beach and its sand quality varies, the sea is very shallow for a long way out, making it popular with young families.

From the main highway, a number of side roads go down to **Almyrós** beach, with two holiday complexes. Further on, don't be put off by the roadside sprawl of tourist facilities at **Aharávi** . The side roads leading to its long beach are lush with olive and citrus trees, giving this relatively new resort much laid-back charm, as does the 'Old Village' on the south side of the road, opposite the water pump.

The neighbouring resort of **Róda** is quite heavily developed but with several older buildings, narrow streets and a pretty little square still surviving among the tavernas, gift shops and touristy bars and restaurants. Remains of a 5th-century BC Doric temple of Apollo have been discovered here, but despite a signpost, there is nothing to see.

The booming resort of **Sidári** , 39km (24 miles) from Kérkyra Town by the most direct road, is by far the most developed on the north coast and its main street reflects many of the less savoury aspects of mass tourism on the island. Nonetheless, a picturesque little village square survives, with a charming church. The

⊙ CHANNEL OF LOVE

The most famous of Sidári's many rock formations is the Canal d'Amour. Legend has it that anyone who swims through this narrow channel (when the water is in shade, according to some versions) will find the man or woman of their dreams. The problem is that the original Canal d'Amour, topped by a sea arch, collapsed long ago, and today nobody can quite decide which is the current Canal d'Amour. If you are in search of love, take no chances and swim through them all.

broad, sandy main beach has very shallow warm water and a wide range of water sports. Sidári's finest feature, however, is the series of striking coastal **rock formations** flanking the resort on the west.

Perouládes panorama

The striated sandstone here is continuously carved by the wind and the sea into sandy coves with caves and ledges (some of which are very good for diving). There are a number of adjacent bays to explore, becoming more spectacular the further west you go. At the last bay you can go no further and, for your own safety, a fence blocks the top of the bluff. The view from here – of the giant cliffs tumbling straight down into the sea – is breathtaking.

From Sidári (and also from Ágios Stéfanos Gýrou), boat trips run to the three small islets lying to the northwest, known collectively as the **Diapóndia Islands**. Going clockwise, these are Mathráki, Othoní and Eríkousa, and are famous both for their fishing grounds and fervent Italian patronage. **Othoní** is the largest and most mountainous, and the westernmost point of Greece, and is occasionally visited as a day trip from Ágios Stéfanos only, along with hilly, green **Mathráki**, the smallest islet, but with a long, sandy beach. **Eríkousa** has a pair of excellent sandy beaches and attracts the most visitors, from Sidári especially. Each island has at least one taverna and one place (often more) to stay overnight but you'll have to reserve well in advance for summer.

Stunning views of the northwestern tip of Corfu await at **Peouládes** ㉘, 2km (1.2 miles) west of Sidári. Follow signs through the village for **Longás** beach; from the car park at the road's-end, a flight of steps leads down to this narrow, but eminently scenic beach at the base of sheer, gold-grey striated cliffs. There are no facilities on the beach itself, but the café on the cliff top by the top of the stairs provides a fantastic if expensive place to watch the sunset. From the village, another track leads out to Cape Drástis, the island's northwestern tip, where you'll discover a pretty cove and more interesting offshore rock formations.

THE NORTHWEST

Ágios Stéfanos Gýrou ㉙ (not to be confused with Ágios Stéfanos Sinión on the east coast), also called San Stefano, is a popular family resort with a long, wide beach of compacted sand and pebbles ending at white cliffs. West of the resort, excursion boats and scheduled ferries depart from the fishing harbour to the Diapóndia Islands. From the port, a path leads out onto Cape Kefáli, the westernmost point of Corfu.

A 45 minute cliff-top walk to the south (or a roundabout inland drive) leads to **Arílas** in the next bay. This low-key resort is less developed than its neighbour – perhaps because the gently shelving beach is much smaller and narrower.

Easily the finest, and best-protected beach in the far northwest lies beyond yet another headland (Cape Aríla) at **Ágios Geórgios Págon** ㉚: a long (2km/1.2 miles) crescent of coarse

> ### Alkinoos's palace
>
> Many claim that Paleokastrítsa was the site of the reputedly fabulous palace of the Homeric King Alkinoös. Its magnificent setting is indeed fit for a king.

sand. Water sports (including scuba diving) are available, and the water is deep and clean. There are stunning views over the bay from the cliffs at Afiónas, a picturesque village on the sheltering headland that ends at a little lighthouse.

PALEOKASTRÍTSA

You can reach the most celebrated beauty spot on the island by a fast, paved road from Kérkyra Town; the distance is 25km (16 miles). During the 1820s **Paleokastrítsa** ㉛ was a favourite picnic spot for High Commissioner Sir Frederick Adam, and it is said that he had the first road built across Corfu especially to reach it. (To justify the expense he proposed constructing a military convalescent home there, but it was never built.)

Paleokastrítsa's monastery

Several small coves with incredibly clear turquoise water nestle in a coastline of hills and promontories draped in olive, cypress and lemon trees. Strips of partly sandy, partly shingle beach ring the shoreline, and sea grottoes yawning out of sheer cliffs provide employment for the local boatmen who ferry visitors to and fro. Some way south in the sea, a large ship-shaped rock known as Kolóvri is said to be the petrified Phaeacian ship that once bore Ulysses home.

'Paleó', as it is sometimes called, was never a village as such, but merely the port of the Lákones just uphill. The year-round population is said to be less than 50, but this is hard to

Exploring the sea caves

believe during the high season, when several hundred Corfiots move down from their hillside homes to cater for the crowds that flock to this scenic spot.

Fortunately, no building has been permitted to crowd the bright little **monastery of Theotókou** (daily 9am–1pm and 3–8pm) that perches on the main, wooded promontory. You must dress appropriately to enter, and suitable wraps are provided at the gate for women. Established during the 13th century after the discovery here of an icon of the Mother of God (Theotókou), the monastery was rebuilt following a fire in the 18th century. Today it is a lovely, peaceful haven, and many thousands of photographs have been taken of its delightful patio, where a picturesque, creamy-yellow, typically Ionian bell tower decked with pink bougainvillea is set off by a brilliant blue sky. Its three bells represent the Holy Trinity. Visit in the evening when there are few visitors and the soft light is at its best.

A tiny museum harbours ancient icons (the best a St George by 17th-century Cretan master Theodoros Poulakis), vestments and various oddities, including an old olive press, huge wine barrels, a giant clam and some enormous bones – 'part of the skeleton of a huge sea monster which was killed by the crew of a French ship in 1860 in the waters by the monastery', enthuses the caption on the latter item. The poor creature was in fact probably a whale. As you enter the monastery church, you may be given a candle to light; a donation, or patronage of the monastery shop, is expected.

Paleó's main beach of Ágios Spyrídon is the most crowded, but is the departure point for boat excursions to Corfu's only sea caves and grottoes, with their mysterious pink rocks and blue 'eyes' – extremely deep holes that, with the play of sunlight, turn an incredibly deep blue colour. A longer trip can be made north from Paleokastrítsa to Ágios Geórgios Págon – a beautiful voyage, chugging past jagged cliffs that dwarf your tiny vessel. If you are lucky, you might see the dolphins that often cavort in these waters.

The finest view of Paleokastrítsa is from the precariously perched balcony-village of **Lákones**, high above the coastline and accessed by a twisty paved road, or a marked path. A little further on, at a café called – with some understatement – Bella Vista, is a magnificent panorama that ranks among the finest in Europe; in pre-café days, this was a favourite picnic spot for High Commissioner Adam and his Corfiot wife.

From Paleokastrítsa ('Little Old Castle') you can easily reach **Angelókastro** ❷ (Mon–Fri May–Sept 8.30am–2.45pm, extra hours as funding permits, gate often open), which may have been built during the 12th century by Byzantine Emperor Manuel I Komnenos; it certainly existed by 1272, when Norman raiders from Sicily took it briefly. In 1537 several thousand Corfiots held out against Ottoman attack in this nearly impregnable citadel.

From the car park at the foot of the castle, itself reached via the unpopulated hamlet of Kríni, it is an easy, 10-minute climb to the summit with its little church of Ágios Ioánnis and some mysterious rock-cut graves adjacent. Little else is left inside the walls, beyond some cisterns, but the views from here are marvellous – it was a strategic watchpoint over the sea lanes to Italy, and in visual communication with Kérkyra Town's Old Fort.

Backtrack through Kríni to **Makrádes** ㉝, where the main road is lined with souvenir stalls and tavernas catering to tour buses. The village itself (off a side road to the left) is a brightly whitewashed cluster of houses with many picturesque corners. Just beyond Makrádes, follow the steep, but completely paved road to **Pági**. The first reward is the stunning vista of Ágios Geórgios Bay you get before you arrive. The second is the peaceful mountain village itself, crowned by an Ionian belfry.

Alternatively, you can join the main trans-island road at the **Troumbétas Pass**. *Troumbétas* means 'trumpet', and the pass is so called after the musically minded officer in charge of the road construction team who liked to stand on the pass above and blow a trumpet to call the crew to lunch. From here you can head north to Sidári or Róda, or return to Kérkyra Town via Skriperó.

THE WEST

The wide Rópa Valley opens out just inland from Paleokastrítsa and its gateway village of Gardeládes. This former marsh was drained by the Italians during their brief occupation in World War II, and is now the island's agricultural heartland. South of Rópa, along the west coast, lie Corfu's best beaches, with wide stretches of deep, golden sand.

The Rópa river flows down through the valley and out to the sea at **Érmones**, making it the main contender for the site

Glyfáda's long sandy beach, one of the finest on the west coast

where Odysseus was found by Nausika and her retinue. The bay is picturesque, but its small (100m/330ft wide) beach of sand and pebble is not particularly attractive and is hemmed in by hotel and bungalow developments. The main hotel runs a somewhat rickety funicular service down to the beach.

By contrast, **Myrtiótissa** ③④ was described by Lawrence Durrell, over 80 years ago, as 'perhaps the loveliest beach in the world', but today it is perhaps the most overrated beach on Corfu. Although the access road (signposted at Kelliá village, near Pélekas) is now paved, it is still dauntingly steep as it worms its way down forested cliffs, and except in spring or autumn, parking is hopeless (there is a car-park of sorts up by the handy Bella Vista taverna, and the local monastery, as well as turning leeway). Most days, the beach is a diamond-shaped lozenge of sand at best 28m (90ft) broad, with offshore boulders to baffle the waves and several drink, trinket and umbrella stalls compounding the space problem. It's usually wall-to-wall, uniformly naked bodies here, as this is the island's designated naturist cove – just barely out of sight from the 14th-century **monastery of Myrtiótissa**, uphill to the north (doorbell not answered; arrange admission via www.mirtidiotissa.com).

Adjacent to Myrtiótissa as the seagull flies, but via a round-about land route, is a beach more worthy of acclaim, **Glyfáda** ㉟. Against a backdrop of crumbling cliffs with rock formations at either end, this 450-metre stretch of sand is one of the finest on the island, and accordingly popular with day trippers from Kérkyra Town and other resorts – as well as many Greeks and Italians in July. Swimming is superb; the water is initially shallow, but deepens further out. There is often a bit of surf for body boarders, as well as periodic strong undertow at the northern end (as on many beaches along the west coast). Glyfáda is somewhat overwhelmed by two large hotel complexes, but there's no arguing with the four-star sand and amenities (including showers, sunbeds and water sports).

A steep hill leads up from Glyfáda to the village of **Pélekas** ㊱. Today it is busy and commercialised, full of travel agencies, restaurants, cafés and rooms for rent. Nonetheless, it is still an attractive place and makes a good coffee or meal stop – if you can find a parking place. Follow signposts to the famous **Kaiser's Throne**, just above Pélekas on a high ridge. At this panoramic viewpoint, Kaiser Wilhelm II built a small telescope point to watch the spectacular sunsets. From here, at certain times of the year, the sun appears to slide diagonally down the hillside and into the sea. The views at any time are excellent, from Paleokastrítsa in the west to Kérkyra Town in the east.

The closest beach to Pelekás, well signposted below the village, is **Kondogialós**, reached by yet another steep, winding access road. It's actually longer than Glyfáda, at about 700m

(2275ft), though the beach is a bit narrower, with a portion of rocky shore providing good snorkelling in crystal waters. Wooden boardwalks cross the burning sand, and there's some free parking available at the far north end (most west-coast beaches have unavoidable, stiff parking fees collected by roving wardens). Development comprises a handful of tavernas and a large hillside hotel complex.

Sinarádes

The unspoiled hill town of **Sinarádes** ㊲ lies 5km (3 miles) south of Pélekas. Towards the north end of Sinarádes, opposite the Venetian-style church tower, signs point up a stair street to the **History and Folklore Museum of Central Corfu** (May–Oct Tue–Sun 9.30am–2pm). This minimally restored traditional Corfiot house, of a type prevalent between 1860 and 1960, contains two floors crammed with artefacts and documents. The ground floor has been left more or less as it was when inhabited, with cooking and hearth implements in the kitchen plus mocked-up salon and bedroom. The star of the single room topfloor gallery, mostly devoted to farming and craft tools (including a shoemaker's workbench), is a portion of a *papyrélla* raft, made of cane fennel, used along the west and northwest coasts of Corfu until World War II. Other oddities include a moray eel trap, a wicker cage to keep toddlers from wandering off, and two special saddles used by village women when giving birth.

The scenic bay of **Ágios Górdis** ㊳, enclosed by shaggy slopes (but rather dominated by the giant Pink Palace backpackers' complex), is punctuated by a massive pinnacle rising from the water at the southern end – an excellent spot for snorkelling, as are the rocks at the northern end. The 600-metre sand-and-shingle beach, despite being far from the best on Corfu, can get crowded in season, as the resort just inland is sizable.

EXCURSIONS

Both the idyllic islands of Paxí (the ancient Paxos), its dependency Andípaxi and the nearby Greek mainland are easily accessible for day trips out of Kérkyra Town, Lefkímmi and sometimes Benítses. Corfu travel agents can provide you with information on such excursions and on ferry schedules if you wish to stay longer.

PAXÍ

One of the most delightful island experiences in the Mediterranean awaits you just 10 nautical miles south of Corfu. Tiny, verdant **Paxí** ㊴, the smallest of the seven principal Ionian Islands – approximately 11km (7 miles) long and 5km (3 miles) wide – about 19 km sq –has some 300,000 olive trees and about 2,300 permanent residents. It is famous for the quality of its olive oil; to this day Paxí earns almost as much from olives as from

⊙ A CHIP OFF THE OLD BLOCK

According to Greek mythology, the sea god Poseidon created Paxí by striking off the southern part of Corfu to make a retreat for himself and his consort, the sea-nereid Amphitrite.

tourism. This quiet, relatively un-commercialised island is wonderfully tidy – there is virtually no litter or roadside rubbish; while houses, villas, shops and restaurants are maintained and painted as if in preparation for a competition for the best-kept Greek island.

The clear, limpid waters off Paxí are irresistible. The island has no natural sandy beaches, though off shingly Harámi at Lákka the bottom is pure sand. However, you'll find excellent swimming from flat rocks and numerous pebbly coves around the shoreline, even if many are accessible only by boat. There is a small strip of imported sand on the islet of Mogonísi in the far south, but it is nearly always crowded.

Sea caves in the towering cliffs along the west coast are truly spectacular, and the blue water there is so dazzling in its intensity that snorkelling is something you won't soon forget. The sea depth off these sheer rocks plunges from 25m to 90m (82ft to 295ft), with fish of varying sizes gliding along in schools, at different levels. The largest cave, Ypapandí, was said to be a lair of Poseidon. A modern legend has it that a British submarine hid here for many months during World War II, venturing out on occasion to conduct valiant operations. Nearby, Aháï cave is fetchingly side-lit; tour-boats enter both for photo-ops. Soaring out of the sea along this stunning coast is **Orthólithos** – a huge finger of rock that has been hewn out of the cliff face by the elements; weather permitting,

boat trips thread between it and Paxí on their way past the Trypitós rock-arch.

Peaceful Paxí often appeals to those who want to get away from it all. But this can be difficult in midsummer, especially in the first three weeks of August, when the tiny island becomes a magnet for Italian tourists. Then, prices swell accordingly and accommodation is heavily booked. The island has only two large hotel complexes; other accommodation is in fairly upmarket villas and apartments, though visitors who want to stay only a few nights can often find rooms to rent in private houses. However, in high season it's sensible to book well in advance.

As a day tripper, you only get a whistle-stop tour of Paxí (including its sea caves) and Andípaxi, where you don't even go ashore – boats merely anchor for a swim. To do Paxí justice, you should visit on a scheduled ferry and plan to stay at least two nights – enough time to see all the island's highlights and savour its relaxed atmosphere.

From Kérkyra Town, ferries to Paxí all go via Igoumenítsa, but schedules change frequently so enquire at the ferry agencies. The journey takes up to three hours (via Igoumenítsa).

All ferry boats arrive at **Gáïos**, the small quayside capital of the island, named for the disciple of Paul who evangelised Paxí. The pretty waterfront square is lined with tavernas, shops and charming weathered houses, while handsome yachts fill the harbour.

Most excursion boats originate in Corfu Town, but all make a stop at **Lefkímmi** port to take on passengers from the southern resorts. You'll have less time at sea but a cheaper ticket if you board there. Depending on the company and day, your boat will call at either Gáïos or **Lákka,** a pretty port situated around an almost landlocked bay on the northern island shore. It's the island's sailing capital and has numerous cafés and tavernas, plus ample shopping opportunities. This is the first stop for many cruises, and it's best to skip the mediocre swimming at Harámi in favour of a proper, leisurely lunch – on board there is only *souvláki* and drinks. From Lákka there is a pleasant walk to the inland monastery of **Ypapandí**, the oldest on the island, whose bell tower provides scenic views. Day-cruises sail around the northerly tip of Paxí, where an 1829-erected **lighthouse** had to be rebuilt in 1919 after earthquake damage.

Longós (also spelled Loggós) is a quieter east-coast settlement, not visited by excursions, huddled around a lovely harbour with numerous places to eat and drink. Two of the best Paxian beaches – Levréhio and Monodéndri – are also near here.

There is a regular bus service between the three main settlements, though it operates only during the day and early evening. Scooter hire is available. There are a handful of taxis, but it can be difficult (if not impossible) to find one late at night.

Walking around the island is an attractive option. Little-used tracks and paths along stone terraces and

Excursion companies

Kostas Boat Trips tel +30 6945 137630

Ionian Cruises https://ionian-cruises.com

Britannia/Corfu Cruises https://corfucruises.com

through mature olive groves end in idyllic hamlets. Along the roadsides you'll see abandoned stone cottages and old olive presses, as well as lovingly tended grape arbours, cacti and bougainvillea in profusion. The surrounding hillsides are dotted with round stone towers of ruined, mastless windmills.

A popular walk leads from Magaziá, in the centre of the island, up to the tidy hilltop cemetery at the Ágii Apóstoli (Holy Apostles) Church, where there is a striking view of the chalk-coloured Erimítis cliffs.

ANDÍPAXI

Andípaxi ⓴ (Antipaxos) is an undeveloped island less than three nautical miles south of Gáïos; by shuttle-boat the journey takes 30 to 40 minutes. Cloaked in vineyards and lapped by transparent turquoise water, Andípaxi has only a handful of permanent residents, but attracts plenty of visitors who converge on the island's two beaches. Little Vríka cove boasts an arc of fine, white sand, with tavernas at either end and a few beach umbrellas for hire. The nearby bay of Vatoúmi has brilliant-white pebbles along its coastal strip but a soft, sandy bottom underwater; there are tavernas, one on the hillside, one behind the beach. Cruises anchor off of an unamenitied pebble cove, but the swimming is excellent.

Swimming at both Vríka and Vatoúmi is superb, but don't expect to enjoy them in solitude. Excursion *kaïkia* continually drop off bathers throughout the day, and

> ### Giant tree
>
> Between Magaziá and Fondána stands the island's largest olive tree – it takes five men with outstretched arms to embrace the huge twisted trunk. This giant stands in an incredible grove of 500-year-old trees, all still producing fruit faithfully every two years.

numerous private yachts also moor offshore.

PÁRGA AND SÝVOTA

Párga ④ occupies an exquisite seascape on mainland Greece's north-west coast, east of Paxí. Its several consecutive bays are backed by verdant hillsides and dotted by offshore islands. As you arrive by sea, note the tiny island of Panagía, just off Kryonéri beach, crowned by a lonely church.

The crystal blue water off Voutoumi Beach

Like Corfu, this is by no means 'untouched Greece'. Párga has been very commercialised for decades, with a profusion of restaurants, bars and tourist shops, none terribly different from those in Corfu. Yet Párga is still a delight. Its spectacular setting and views and narrow lanes have an appeal all their own.

A Venetian castle built around 1400 on an earlier Norman structure looms above the promontory immediately to the north of the town. The climb up Párga's steep streets to the castle is actually shorter than it looks from below and well worth the effort for the stupendous views. Be sure to follow the lanes around the base of the castle-hill for additional views of the next bay, **Váltos**, fringed by a long, splendid golden-sand beach.

The alternative mainland excursion is to the magnificent coves and seascapes around the otherwise not compelling resort of Sývota e – specifically the sandspit at **Bélla Vráka, Zaviás** beach and lagoon-like **'Piscine'**.

Strolling around Corfu Town's pretty streets

WHAT TO DO

SHOPPING

Greece is now one of the more expensive Mediterranean destinations, so don't expect bargains on Corfu – except perhaps during the August sales. In souvenir shops some good-natured bargaining may be tolerated if you are buying more than one item or spending a reasonable amount, but don't push it. Local profit margins have to cover not only the tourist months, but also the off-season when most shops close, and some shops even put up signs saying 'Fixed Prices' or 'No Bargaining'.

If you are not a resident of the EU, you might be able to claim back the 24 percent VAT (sales tax) included in the price, but only if you spend over €120 in one day at a shop participating in the scheme –on Corfu, few do.

WHERE TO SHOP

By far the best range and quality of goods on the island are to be found in Kérkyra Town. Here, the elegant old-world atmosphere of evening shopping (even if you are only window-browsing) is not to be missed. There are also a number of specialist outlets on the road from Kérkyra Town to Paleokastrítsa or Róda.

BEST BUYS

Gifts from the olive tree. Corfu's most plentiful commodity – olive-wood prunings – provides the basis for many fine souvenirs. Local artisans carve attractive bowls, platters, trays, utensils, statuettes, jewellery, toys and other ingenious olive-wood oddities. The most important consideration is that the wood be properly cured (ideally for three years); craftsmen find greener wood easier to work,

Corfiot villages produce handmade lace and embroidery

but once home, green-wood bowls and cutting boards quickly develop horrendous cracks. Also, avoid glued-together cutting boards. One shop patronised repeatedly, with good results, is Kostas Avlonitis' Art of Olive Wood (www.olive-wood.gr/corfu). The island's olives, olive paste and high-quality olive oil are appreciated worldwide; a small bar of olive-oil soap, tastefully gift wrapped, is an ideal, inexpensive present. The Patounis Soap Factory on Sarokko plaza is the place for this.

Pottery and ceramics. Corfu is home to many talented potters. You'll come across some lovely ceramics, including museum copies (the shop in Kérkyra Town's Old Fort specialises in these, as well as official, high-quality archaeological publications).

Gold and silver. Silversmiths still create bowls and trays using centuries-old Greek and Venetian patterns, beating out the silver much as their ancestors would have done. Many of the jewellery designs are based on archetypal symbols from the earliest years of Greek civilisation, including the lion, dolphin, ram and bull. Evgeníou Voulgáreos Street, off the Listón, is the place to find silver in Kérkyra Town.

Leather. Leather handbags, sandals, shoes, gloves, wallets and belts are often very good buys in Kérkyra Town. Agíon Pándon Street is home to many young and creative fashion designers; more traditional outlets are found on Nikifórou Theotókou.

Weaving and embroidery. There's a good selection of hand-woven and embroidered items. Colourful woollen shoulder bags called *tagária*, hand-woven floor mats in muted colours, tablecloths, napkins, aprons, skirts and blouses of lace and cotton (in particular those woven in villages) are popular. Best buys in this category are cotton needlework shawls and bedspreads. Kassiópi is home to a traditional industry of lace and crocheted goods.

Reproduction icons. These are sold across Kérkyra Town and vary greatly in price according to size and quality. Icons are also sold at the monasteries at Mt Pandokrátor and Paleokastrítsa.

Other specialities. Kumquat liqueur is a novelty made from a small southeast Asian citrus fruit grown on Corfu (locally spelled as *koum quat*). There are medium and dry varieties of this sweet, orange-coloured drink, though the white extract is considered the best quality. It, and crystallised kumquat fruit, are sold throughout Corfu, and the Mavromatis factory (https://kumquat.gr) on the Paleokastrítsa road is a popular stop with tour groups.

Another sweet treat worth trying is almond nougat (*mandoláto*). In addition, the rich island flora ensures that honey always possesses a distinctive character. In fruit and vegetable markets, look for bags of herbs and spices.

Corfu has a distinctive item of charcuterie, *noúmboulo* – cured pork tenderloin, eaten raw in thin slices. Any supermarket deli counter will have some, often mediocre, so it's best to buy direct from a reputed producer such as Darmanis, in town at Nikólaou Ventoúra 20, or Mihalas near Doukádes.

Corfu Beer

Corfu has a truly excellent, family-run microbrewery (www.corfubeer.com) near Arílas, producing seven beers including a great red, plus three fruit-flavoured fizzy drinks. Their shop is open daily, though tours are only given Saturdays at midday.

The Corfiots' love of music runs deep

Other typically Greek souvenir ideas include strands of worry beads (*kombologiá*), or a *bríki*, a long-stemmed copper coffee pot used for making Greek coffee, which also makes an attractive mantelpiece ornament.

ENTERTAINMENT

Corfu is indeed a very musical island. Thanks to the Venetian legacy, Kérkyra Town alone boasts three orchestras, with nearly a dozen more spread over the island, representing several hundred musicians in all, as well as a municipal choir and a chamber-music group; historically nearly half the Athens Symphony Orchestra was Corfu Conservatory-trained. Marching brass bands (the somewhat confusingly called *filarmonikés orhístres*) are a regular fixture at festivals, and often give summer Sunday concerts on the Spianáda. Despite current funding problems, summer still sees some festivals, notably the two-day Ágios Ioánnis soul, rock and folk festival (www.agiotfest.com) and Paleokastrítsa's Varkarola Festival in mid-August. Corfu Beer hosts a late-September festival, whose emphasis changes annually, in the fine open space just opposite their premises.

Theatre lovers might attend summer performances (often of ancient Greek plays), either in one of Kérkyra Town's two fortresses or at the Mon Repos outdoor theatre. Other venues for quality events include the auditorium of the Ionian Academy, the somewhat grim Municipal Theatre (a replacement for the one bombed in September 1943), the New Fort, and just outside the latter the Polytechno. For details of all concerts, festivals and theatre pick up a cultural events leaflet from the airport or the local tourist information office. The website http://corfuwall.gr is also very useful.

⊙ LOCAL WINE TASTING

Despite its vineyards being remarked on by ancient writers, Corfu is not among the most distinguished Greek *domaines* – indeed most island wine lists rely on mainland bottles – there are some Corfiot vineyards.

Theotoky Estate (www.theotoky.com) in Rópa Valley near Giannádes, the most known vintner. Organic production of reds, rosés and whites. Tasting by appointment Mon–Sat, shop open daily.

Ambelonas (http://ambelonas-corfu.gr/#wine-gastronomy-culture), just off the road between Corfu Town and Pélekas. Combination vintner's and taverna – the owner is a well-regarded chef. Only open Wed, Thu, Fri and Sun 7–11pm.

Grammenos (http://grammenosfamily-wines.com) at Aerostáto, between Aï Górdis resort and Sinarádes. Produces two whites, a red and a rosé, relying on local varieties like Katotrýgi (white) and Petrokórythos (red), but also uses red grapes imported from the Peloponnese. Tours only by arrangement.

Nikoluzos (http://nicoluzo.com) in Áno Korakiána. A newish (since 2015) small winery rarely topping 10,000 bottles annually. Its signature Gorgo series – white, rosé and red – relies partly on indigenous grape varieties like *anthosmías*. Only found at better tavernas/hotels, not local supermarkets.

Performances of songs and dances occur at village festivals throughout the season (from Pentecost Sunday to late August, look for posters on trees and utility poles), though execution has suffered recently, with costumed dancers and acoustic musicians replaced by casual dress and poor electric bands.

⊙ CORFIOT EASTER

Kérkyra Town stages the most colourful Easter (*Páskha*) celebration in Greece. Here it is also called Lambrí ('brilliance'), and the spectacle attracts throngs of Greeks and foreigners, with all town hotels full for the duration. Each parish has its Good Friday procession of the *epitáfios* or funeral bier of Christ. The best starts after nightfall, departing from the cathedral with the bishop, dignitaries and one of Corfu's famous 'philharmonic' (brass) bands.

On Holy Saturday morning, the body of the patron saint, Spyridon, is paraded at length around town in honour of his miraculous intervention in 1553, which saved Corfu from famine. Then, at 11am, police clear the streets for the *bótídes* rite. Suddenly old plates, vases or clay pots full of water and other breakables are hurled from the upper storeys of houses. The best explanation of this unique Corfu custom, possibly Venetian in origin, is that it banishes misfortune, including Judas' betrayal of Jesus.

The Catholic Easter Saturday evening mass takes place somewhat before the Orthodox one. At midnight, when the Orthodox bishop intones *'Hristós anésti'* ('Christ is risen'), every electric light goes on, fireworks soar overhead, church bells ring and – most memorably – everyone lights a candle. On Easter Sunday at noon, lambs are put to the spit, wine flows like water and men perform traditional dances.

Otherwise, Kérkyra Town hosts 'Cultural Evenings' during summer, at Platía Dimarhíou, Platía Ioniki and the old port plaza in Spiliá, featuring folk dancing, classical music and traditional choral music.

For less formal happenings, look no further than the nearest musical bar or dance club in any major resort like Kávos or Sidári – though in these tough times the emphasis is more on small, often

Easter procession

weekends-only spots like DiZi Beach Bar at Érmones, or Edem Beach Club (https//edemclub.com) in Dassiá. The mega-nightclub strip along the main road (Ethnikís Antistáseos) west of the new port has pretty much withered away since the 2010–11 Greek debt crisis, leaving only 54 Dreamy Nights (www.Facebook/54 Dreamy Nights) as the most durable survivor.

One casino (www.casinocorfu.gr) operates in the Corfu Palace Hotel (8pm–3am; formal dress code; minimum age 23, ID required). It offers roulette, blackjack, baccarat and chemin de fer.

GREEK NIGHTS

During your stay you may come across a 'Greek night', though these are essentially dying out. They generally involve a (more or less) traditional meal, with music and dancing touted as the main attraction. Traditional Corfiot and national Greek dances are taught from an early age, and the dancers – whether specially hired performers, restaurant staff or simply locals doing their bit – can almost always be relied on for an energetic performance.

Corfiot men revel in athletic, fast dances with high-kicking steps evincing bravado. Dancing in a ring of fire to the accompaniment of plate-smashing is typical. Another stunt involves picking up a glass of wine with the mouth from a press-up position. The wine is downed with a jerk of the neck; more macho types bite a chunk out of the empty glass before tossing it contemptuously aside. Another crowd-pleaser has a dancer bending back to apparently pick up a heavy table only with his teeth (he's actually taking the table's weight on his chest and stomach). Expert practitioners extend this feat to a table with a chair on top, and some go for broke by getting a young child to sit on the chair.

By the end of the evening, the dancers will probably have cajoled everyone onto the floor to join in a version of the *syrtáki*, Greece's best-known line dance; steps are simplified for visitors. Accompaniment is usually provided by a *bouzoúki*, which has become synonymous with all Greek music. In fact, the instrument (of Middle Eastern origin) is a very recent import to the island, though the popular melodies of Manos Hatzidakis, Mikis Theodorakis and the great composers of *rebétika* have made it an intrinsic part of Greek heritage.

Renting a boat

The best way to enjoy the coastline is by boat. You can rent all types of motorboats, from a small outboard to a 10m (33ft) *caique*. One popular northeast-coast operator is Agni Boats (www.agni boats.com).

SPORTS AND RECREATION

Snorkelling and diving. Clear, salubrious sea laps Corfu's innumerable rocky inlets, and you will find small, fascinating grottoes and offshore rocks near Paleokastrítsa, Sidári, Perouládes, Othoní and Paxí. Paleokastrítsa is considered to be one of Europe's best diving locations, with visibility up to 30 metres, though the water can be chilly year-round. The most impressive local site is the Hole of Ha, a sea-cave penetrating some distance inland; the ceiling has partially collapsed, so

Parasailing in Dassia

that at midday sunlight pours in. A day-long outing to Othoní visits two wrecks and another cave, while advanced divers enjoy the two caves of western Paxí and a deep (40m) wreck. Don't be put off by Neptune grass at certain east-coast points; beds of the plant (*Posidonia oceanica*) serve as a nursery and browsing ground for many colourful fish, and indicate lack of pollution.

Scuba-diving schools have qualified instructors who will choose dive locations according to the amount of experience you have, and conditions on the day. The following reputable schools operate in northern Corfu:

Achilleion Diving, Agía Triáda cove, Paleokastrítsa (tel: 26630 42023, www.diving-corfu.com), with conscientious staff and sound equipment; €89 for a two-dive half-day nearby, €140 expedition to Othoní, €380 for an open-water PADI certification (4 days).

Dive Easy, Aharávi and Imeroliá port, Kassiópi (tel: 26630 29350, www.diveeasygr.com), using a solid-hull (not RIB) boat;

two northeast coast dives, €85; expedition to Othoní, €100; open-water PADI course, €400.

Apollo Dive Centre, Nissáki (tel: 6974705697, https://apollosub.com), closest to an assortment of northeast coast reefs and wrecks; prices unavailable but likely competitive.

Water sports. Dassiá and Ýpsos are established water sports centres. Windsurfing equipment is available for hire at many beaches on the island where the right conditions prevail, and instruction is offered at many places. Parasailing is available at several beaches, as is kitesurfing; there's a dedicated kite school at Halikoúnas beach (www.kite-club-korfu.com).

Golf. The acclaimed Corfu Golf Club (tel: 26610 94220; www.corfu-golfclub.com), in the Rópa Valley near Érmones, is rated as one of the best in the Mediterranean. The 18-hole course features water hazards and provides real challenges for seasoned golfers. You can arrange lessons via the website; clubs and other essentials are available for hire. You'll also find a good shop and clubhouse with a bar and restaurant.

Hiking. Corfu is a good place for avid walkers who may follow a 220-km-long route – some of it path, much of it track – along the length of the island, taking about 10 days to complete. Summer is too hot, and water/camping space en route is scarce. Check www.thecorfutrail.com for details.

Horse riding. There are two bona fide stables on the island: Arena Horse Riding near Ágios Spyrídon beach (https://horseridingcorfu.com) with rides around the Andinióti lagoon and long-established Trailriders in Áno Korákiana (www.trailriderscorfu.com), offering two-hour morning or evening rides, Monday to Friday, in season.

Cricket. Cricket was introduced by the English and remains an integral part of Corfu's summer scene. Matches take place at the cricket ground at Gouviá Marina on Saturday and Sunday afternoons. Corfu clubs frequently play against visiting teams from

Britain and Malta. There is another pitch at the Corfu Golf Club in Rópa Valley, while youth teams play at the pitch on the Spianáda in Kérkyra Town.

ACTIVITIES FOR CHILDREN

Corfu is a very popular family holiday spot. Larger hotels have separate, shallow children's swimming pools and play areas, and most have limited-hour crèches and/or 'kids' clubs' with a full range of activities.

Corfu has many beaches suited to young children

While most beaches are perfectly safe for children, those with sandy shores and/or very shallow water will appeal most to families with very young children. These include Róda, Sidári, Aharávi, Ágios Stéfanos Gýrou, Arílas, Moraïtika, Mesongí and Marathiá.

The most popular children's day out (and a great day for all splashaholics) is at the Aqualand water park (www.aqualand-corfu.com), with many thrill rides, a gentle 'Lazy River', the bouncy castle, swimming pools and special children's play area. Located at Ágios Ioánnis in the centre of the island, some 12km (7.5 miles) west of Kérkyra Town, the park is open daily (10am–6pm) from May to October. Children under four are admitted free and reduced rates apply after 3pm.

If your children love nature and horses, take them pony-trekking, a good outing for the whole family. This can be booked through most tourist agencies.

CALENDAR OF EVENTS

1 January St Basil's Day (Agíou Vassilíou, Protohroniá). At midnight on New Year's Eve, adults play cards for money and a cake (the vassilópita) with a lucky coin baked into it is cut.

6 January Epiphany (Ta Ágia Theofánia or Ta Fóta). In seaside parishes the priest or bishop blesses the waters by throwing a crucifix into the sea; young men dive to retrieve it; the winner is lucky for the year ahead.

February/March Apókries. Carnival Season of three weekends, prior to Lent. Fancy-dress parties, parades with floats and bands, and (on the third Sunday), the trial and cremation of 'King Carnival'.

'Clean Monday' First day of Orthodox Lent (Katharí Deftéra). In good weather everyone goes on rural outings for a picnic and kite flying.

11 February St Theodora Augusta (Agía Theodóra Avgoústa). The saint's relics are carried in a procession around Kérkyra Town.

25 March Greek Independence Day: procession in Kérkyra Town.

Good Friday Biers form a procession through Kérkyra Town.

Easter Saturday Procession of St Spyridon's coffin around Kérkyra.

Easter Sunday Fireworks and noisy celebrations with music and dance.

1 May May Day/Labour Day. Workers' parades and excursions to the countryside to gather flowers and greenery for May wreaths.

21 May Ionian Union Day (Énosis ton Eptaníson) marks the anniversary of the seven islands joining Greece in 1864.

17 July Agía Marína. Festivities at Avliótes, Benítses, Sparterá and in Sarokko Square, Kérkyra Town.

11 August Feast day in honour of St Spyridon in Kérkyra Town, including procession of St Spyrídon's coffin.

15 August Kímisis tis Theotókou (Dormition of the Mother of God). Festivals at many churches.

1st Sunday in November Procession of St Spyridon's coffin around Kérkyra Town.

12 December St Spyridon Day (Agíou Spyrídonos). Ágios Spyrídon church is open for 24 hours continuously from the eve of 11 December, with ongoing liturgy and a steady stream of pilgrims.

EATING OUT

Take an idyllic waterside setting, add charcoal-grilled fish, meat on a spit and a crisp salad, and you have the basic components of a typical Greek meal. Olive oil, tomatoes, onion, garlic, cheese and lemon are all essentials of a simple cuisine, though Corfu – owing largely to its Venetian heritage – has a few more elaborate dishes unique to the island, and unusually for Greece local cooking features spicy recipes.

The true *estiatório*, restaurants where pre-cooked dishes have equal or superior billing to grilled items, are common only in Kérkyra Town; in these places it's still customary to inspect simmering casseroles on the range and point to your choice. In the resorts, the taverna – with mostly outdoor seating, and thus usually shut from late October to early May – reigns supreme, and ordering by sight is not the rule. But neither should you rely on menus – many of these are wishful thinking, issued free to the establishment by a sponsoring drinks company, listing dishes that are never offered. The only reliable bill of fare will be recited by your waiter; check the menu only to verify prices. These include service charge, but diners

Alfresco dining on the beach

normally leave 5 to 10 percent extra for the waiter. An obligatory cover charge includes bread, which varies in quality – darker village bread is excellent. You may decline it.

Corfiots, like most Greeks, enjoy their food warm rather than piping hot. Casserole dishes such as *moussakás* are cooked for lunchtime and either kept warm all day or just reheated at night. If you like your food hot or if you are concerned about the hygiene implications of re-heating, order only grilled dishes in the evening.

Islanders have lunch between 2.30 and 4pm, dinner from 9.30pm onwards, with many establishments taking last orders as late as 11.30pm. Tavernas aimed at foreigners begin dinner service at around 7pm; you will have your choice of table then, but the atmosphere is definitely better later.

WHAT TO EAT

Fast food

For snacks or even lunch, pop into a bakery for a *tyrópita* (cheese-filled *filo* pastry pie); the *filo*-less version looking like a turnover, called *kouroú*, is less messy and more cheese-filled; if it's stuffed with spinach, it's a *spanakópita*.

Another cheap takeaway option is *gýros*, better known to western Europeans as *doner kebab*. Pressed pork is sliced off a vertically rotating spit

Chicken kebab

and stuffed into *píta* bread with some garnish, *tzatzíki* and a handful of chips. Alternatively there is *souvláki*: charcoal-grilled cubes of pork or lamb served in the same fashion. *Souvláki* is also served as a main sit-down course in tavernas.

Appetisers

Carefully selected appetisers (*orektiká*) can constitute a full meal. Shared by the

> ### Varied cuisine
>
> If you tire of local fare, you can usually find everything from gourmet cuisine to ethnic fare, from Chinese stir-fry to crêpes. Don't turn your nose up at Italian food in particular – the Greeks love pizza and pasta, and the numerous Italian visitors demand high standards in summer.

whole table, they are a fun way to eat – you have as little or as much as you want and keep ordering until you have had your fill.

The most common appetisers are *tzatzíki*, a yoghurt dip flavoured with garlic, cucumber and mint; *dolmádes*, vine leaves stuffed with rice, onions and herbs – rarely mince – which can be served hot (with egg-lemon sauce) or cold (with yoghurt); pale (not pink) *taramosaláta*, cod-roe paste blended with breadcrumbs, olive oil and lemon juice; *skordaliá*, garlic-and-potato sauce served with fried vegetable slices or battered fish; *melitzanosaláta*, a purée of grilled aubergine, onions, olive oil and garlic, preferably *nistísimo* (without mayonnaise); *tyrokafterí*, a spicy cheese dip; and *hórta*, boiled wild greens. *Saganáki* is hard cheese coated in breadcrumbs and then fried, though confusingly the term can also mean a cheese-based red sauce used over mussels and shrimp.

Greek salad or *horiátiki saláta* (usually translated as 'village salad') consists of tomato, cucumber, onion, green peppers and olives topped with feta cheese. Cruets of olive oil and wine vinegar are found with other condiments on the table.

Grilled seafood

Fish and seafood

The seas around Corfu have been overfished and prices for fresh fare are likely to shock many visitors. These are often quoted by weight, so to avoid any unpleasant surprises at the end of your meal, watch the fish being weighed (uncleaned) and confirm the weight to avoid fiddles. If the seafood is frozen or farmed (very likely from June to September), this must by law be stated on the menu – though often only in the Greek-language column, or simply with an asterisk.

Larger fish is usually grilled and smaller fish fried. The most common big species, served with fresh lemon and *ladolémono* (olive oil with lemon juice), are listed in our menu reader, see page 104; watch out also for several tasty varieties of bream, such as *melanoúri* (saddled bream) or *sargós* (white bream). *Barboúni* (red mullet) is also a popular fish on Corfu, while *fangrí* (large bream), and *synagrída* (dentex) are expensive treats.

Marídes (picarel), *gávros* (anchovy) and *sardélles* (sardines) are served crisp-fried, as are *kalamarákia* (baby squid). More elaborate seafood dishes include *okhtapódi krasáto*, octopus stewed in red wine and tomato sauce; *soupiá* (cuttlefish) with spinach-rice; or *garídes* (prawns) in saganáki sauce.

A Corfiot seafood speciality is piquant *bourdéto*: white-fleshed fish stewed with tomatoes, hot red pepper, onions, garlic and olive oil. *Biánko* is, as the name suggests, a 'white' (tomato-less) fish stew with lots of garlic, potatoes, white wine, lemon, oil, black pepper and onions.

Meat and casserole dishes

Sit-down barbecued dishes include whole chickens or *kondosoúvli* (rotisserie-grilled pork). If you want a basic pork or veal cutlet, ask for *brizóla*; lamb chops, however, are *païdákia*.

The Greeks love lamb. *Kléftiko* is oven-roasted lamb, though in Corfu the dish might be served in a sauce of wine, vegetables and yoghurt. Another popular lamb dish is *arní frikassé*, stewed with green vegetables. Even more common is *stámna*: lamb or beef baked in a clay vessel with cinnamon, cloves, sweet pepper and mixed vegetables.

Greece's most famous slow-cooked oven dish is probably *moussakás* – sliced layers of potato, aubergine and minced beef topped with a generous layer of béchamel sauce. It should be firm, but succulent and aromatic with nutmeg; good restaurants make a fresh batch daily. Other common casseroles include *kokinistó* or *stifádo*, braised meat – beef or rabbit – with baby onions.

Sofríto is a Corfiot speciality comprising of slices of beef or veal stewed in a sauce of white wine, garlic and wine vinegar with a touch of black pepper and parsley.

Pasta dishes

Corfiots are very fond of pasta. *Pastítsio* (macaroni pie) is just that, a mixture of macaroni with mince, spices and bechamel sauce. *Giouvétsi* is meat (usually lamb) and *krithαráki* pasta (identical to Italian *orzo*), baked in a clay casserole. Don't confuse *pastítsio* with the local *pastitsáda*, which is either cockerel or lobster chunks in richly flavoured sauce atop thick, round, brown noodles.

Vegetables

Vegetarians should usually find *hórta* (wild chicory greens or cultivated amaranth); *gígandes* (giant butter beans) in sauce; or *fasolákia* (string/runner beans) on menus. For a more substantial hot meatless dish, *gemistá* are tomatoes or peppers stuffed with herb-flavoured rice (though meat stock may be used); alternatively, *melitzánes imám* (aubergine stuffed richly with tomato, onions and oil) is reliably vegetarian, as is *briám* or *tourloú* (a ratatouille of aubergines, potatoes and courgettes). Particularly Corfiot is *tsigarélli*, greens (preferably wild, or chard) sautéed with hot chilli powder and other spices.

Desserts

Most tavernas bring a plate of seasonal fresh fruit as a finale to your meal; Corfu's magnificent wild strawberries *(fráoules)* are harvested in May and June. However, during summer the only fruits that appear on the restaurant table are Persian melons, watermelons and grapes.

For something more unhealthily sweet, the *zaharoplastío* (sticky-cake shop, mostly in Kérkyra Town) offer incredibly decadent oriental sweets: *baklavás*, layers of honey-soaked filo pastry with walnuts; *kataïfi*, 'shredded wheat' filled with chopped almonds and honey; *galaktoboúreko*, custard pie; or *ravaní*, honey-soaked sponge cake. If you prefer dairy desserts, try yoghurt topped with local honey (*méli*); *kréma* (custard); *ryzógalo*, cold rice pudding; or *pagotó* (ice cream) at a number of speciality Kérkyra Town parlours (like Papagiorgis at Nikifórou Theotóki 32) and in many resorts.

WHAT TO DRINK

Alcoholic drinks

Corfu produces a reasonable quantity of wine, but much of this is kept back for private use. Often light red (*kokkinéli*) or deep purple in colour, it is best drunk cool from the cellar. It ranges in quality from almost undrinkable to good-value tippling; always sample a glass first.

Otherwise, choose from the wide range of mainland Greek wines. Three top-drawer, medium-priced reds are Ktima Papaïoannou, Tsantali Rapsani and almost anything from Nemea. For a premium white, try Gentilini Robola from neighbouring Kefaloniá, Spyropoulos, Tselepos and Skouras from the Peloponnese, and Lazaridi from Macedonia.

Numerous beer labels are produced in Greece, including by microbreweries as well as imports. Foreign brands made under licence include

Melitzánes imám

Amstel, Kaiser and Heineken; nationwide labels are Fix (reckoned the best), Alfa, Mammos, Mythos, Pils Hellas and Vergina.

Anise-flavoured *oúzo* is taken as an aperitif with ice and water; a compound in the anise flavouring makes the mix turn harmlessly cloudy. The most popular brands (like Mini, Varvagianni and Plomari) come from Lésvos Island. *Tsípouro* is a north-mainland variant of this grape-mash distillate, best without anise, and popular on Corfu.

The local speciality liqueur is *koum kouat* (kumquat). For a digestif, Metaxa is the most popular domestic brandy, sold (in ascending order of strength and aging) in 3-, 5- and 7-star grades. Mavrodaphne is a fortified red dessert wine similar to Marsala.

Non-alcoholic drinks

Hot coffee (*kafés*) is typically *ellínikós* (generic Middle Eastern style, renamed 'Greek' from 'Turkish' in a fit of patriotism after the various Cyprus crises), freshly brewed in copper pots and served in small cups. It will probably arrive *glykós* (very sweet) unless you order *métrios* (medium) or *skétos* (without sugar); it's always accompanied by a glass of chilled water. Don't drink to the bottom as that's where the grounds settle.

Instant coffee is generically known as *nes* or *néskafe*, irrespective of brand; it's pretty unpalatable, an extra-strength

⊙ GINGER BEER

Kérkyra Town (and Paxí) are the only places in Greece where you can get genuine 19th-century-style ginger beer, a delightful relic of British colonial rule. Locally called *tsitsibýra* (pronounced 'tsi-tsi-BEE-ra'), it should be served well chilled and is extremely refreshing in hot weather.

Ouzo

formula for Mediterranean tastes. There has been a recent backlash against it, so in large resorts and Kérkyra Town you can easily find proper brewed coffee (*gallikós* or *fíltro*), as well as competently executed cappuccino and espresso. *Fredduccino* – cold cappuccino – is also increasingly popular. Any milky coffee (though never with *ellinikós*) is *me gála*.

Frappés, cold instant coffee whipped up in a blender with sugar and milk is quite a fashionable drink. The milky version looks a little like a small Guinness and tastes like a coffee milkshake, but it's surprisingly refreshing in hot weather.

Soft drinks come in all the international varieties, while juices are most likely out of cardboard cartons. Bottled (*enfialoméno*) still mineral water is typically from Crete or the Greek mainland mountains. Souroti and Epsa are the most common domestic sparkling brands. Soda water is usually Tuborg.

TO HELP YOU ORDER...

Could we have a table? **Boroúme na éhoume éna trapézi?**

May we order, please? **Na parangiloúme, parakaló?**

Bon appétit **Kalí órexi**

I'm a vegetarian **Íme hortofágos**

I'm a vegan **Móno tró nistísima piáta**

I have an allergy to... **Ého allergía se...**

The bill, please **To logariazmó, parakaló**

Cheers (as a toast) **Yiámas**

A litre/a half litre **Éna kiló/misó kilo**

Enjoy the rest of your meal (literally, 'Good continuation')
   Kalí synnéhia

plate **piáto**	butter **voútyro**
napkin **hartopetséta**	sugar **záhari**
cutlery **maheropírouna**	salt **aláti**
glass **potíri**	pepper **pipéri**
bread **psomí**	oil **ládi**

...AND READ THE MENU

fried **tiganitó**	chicken **kotópoulo**
baked **sto foúrno**	lamb **arní**
roasted **psitó**	goat **katsíki**
grilled **sta kárvouna**	rabbit **kounélli**
stuffed **gemistá**	salad **saláta**
fish **psári**	tomatoes **domátes**
small shrimp **garídes**	olives **eliés**
octopus **okhtapódi**	boiled greens **hórta**
swordfish **xifías**	cheese **tyrí**
meat **kréas**	wine **krasí**
meatballs **keftedákia**	beer **býra**
beef, veal **moskhári**	(chilled) water **(pagoméno)**
pork **hirinó**	**neró**

PLACES TO EAT

Most restaurants outside of Kérkyra Town close between late October and late April inclusive; we've indicated exceptions, as well as cases where reservations are recommended. All restaurant interiors are non-smoking by law (though some provide ashtrays to indicate non-compliance); if you wish to smoke overtly, this must usually be done outside. The following price ranges reflect the average cost of a two-course meal (per person) and a beer or share of bottled wine, ouzo or tsípouro. These costs include VAT (sales tax), currently 13 percent on food, 24 percent on alcohol, and notional service charge. Unless indicated otherwise, all establishments accept card payment.

€€€€	over 45 euros
€€€	35–45 euros
€€	22–35 euros
€	under 22 euros

KÉRKYRA TOWN

Bakalogatos € *Alypíou 23, corner Prosaléndou, Spiliá district, tel: 26613 01721.* Mon–Sat from midday until 1.30am. 'The grocery cat' emphasises local products – including only Greek wine and microbrewery beer– plus keen prices to draw crowds to its indoor/outdoor tables. The menu is mostly vegetarian including starters such as green peppers stuffed with cheese as well as pork-based recipes such as tiganiá.

Khryssomallis (Babis) € *Nikifórou Theotókou 6, tel: 26610 30342.* Daily noon–10.30pm. The sign says *zythopsitopolío* ('beer-hall-grill'), but it's actually the last traditional oven-food place in the Old Town: stews, *hórta*, *moussakás*, stuffed cabbage leaves, lentil soup and so forth, accompanied by smooth but potent red or rosé wine. From the outside street tables you can just see the Listón. The Durrells ate here during their 1930s stay; the restaurant has been around even longer. Cash only.

La Famiglia €€ *Maniarízi & Arlióti 16 (Kandoúni Bízi), alley between Filellínon and Nikifórou Theotóki*, tel: 26610 30270. Mon–Sat 7.30pm–12.15am, Sun in August, closed Sun/Mon winter. Efficiently run Greek/Italian bistro specialising in salads, pasta dishes like linguine all cozze, a few token Greek platters such as leek pie, and Italian desserts. Excellent bulk wine from Neméa or Santoríni. Limited seating, so reservations always essential.

Mouragia €€ *Arseníou 15, Mourágia quay*, tel: 26610 33815. Apr–Nov noon–12.30am. A good mix of seafood such as flash-fried *atherína* (sand smelt) or sardines and Corfiot specialities such as *sofríto* and *pastitsáda*, plus competent starters at this seaside ouzerí – though views to the sea, and Vídos islet, are over the road.

Psarakia tis Garitsas €€ *Alkiviádou Darí 7, Anemómylos strip*, tel: 26610 30306. Popular, quick-serving seafood place with parkside outdoor tables facing Corfu Town's southerly bay through intervening eucalypts. Excellent squid and great bread for scooping dips. Open inside during winter.

Rouvas € *Stamatíou Desýlla 13*, tel: 26610 31182, www.rouvasrestaurant.com. Mon–Sat 11am–5pm all year. A classic lunchtime hangout that attracts visiting celebrity chefs like Rick Stein to see just how traditional island cooking should be. Recipes include *pastítsio*, artichokes with peas, meat stews, fish soup and grilled mixed vegetables. Unlike many such places, it has a cheery, appealing interior often still crowded at 4pm. Cash only.

Salto Wine Bar Bistro €€ *Dónzelot 23, Spiliá*, tel: 26613 02325, http://saltowinebar.gr. Open nightly all year until midnight (plus Sun lunch). Inspirational cuisine is on offer from chefs Pavlos and Natasha. Fishy dishes, particularly daily specials, include tuna fillets in ginger sauce and seafood kritharotó. Carnivores may enjoy beef fillet or rack of lamb. Save room for dessert of the day. As you'd expect there is a premium Greek wine list.

Tsipouradiko € *Prosaléndou 8–10, behind the Efetío (Appeals Court), Spiliá*, tel: 26610 82240. Mon–Sat 1pm–2am (kitchen shuts 12.30am). Tsípouro is a distilled grape-pomace spirit, preferably without anise, accompanied here by such platters as grilled mushrooms, courgette pie, *tigania* (pork stir-fry), little fishes and aubergine specialities. There is also decent bulk wine. The place is always packed with students and the bohemian set thanks to the warm atmosphere and friendly prices. Smoking allowed in the upstairs loft, or outside in the summer courtyard. Large groups must reserve, or endure a long wait.

Venetian Well €€€€ *Platía Kremastí, northeast of Orthodox Cathedral, Campiello district, tel: 26615 50955, www.venetianwell.gr. Apr–Oct Mon–Sat 7–11.30pm.* Served to summertime tables set around the eponymous well is some of the town's most creative cuisine. Lighter mid-summer menus might feature *glykádia* (sweetbreads) in sauce, scallops, burrata, mushroom-and-goat-cheese mousse; slow-cooked veal cheeks glazed with ginger, lemon grass and honey, with kumquat ice cream to finish. The elegant, interior gets used in cooler months. Excellent, (mostly Greek) wine list from €30 per bottle.

THE SOUTH

Alonaki Bay €€ *Paralía Alonáki, near Korissíon Lagoon and Gardíki Castle, tel: 26610 75872.* Open daily Apr–Oct lunch and dinner. Good country recipes, strong on vegetables and seafood, served at shady tables on a sea view terrace. Their version of *biánko*, with *kéfalos* (grey mullet) hygienically raised in the lake and garnished with marsh samphire (*Salicornia europaea*), is unique. If you can't tear yourself away from this lovely spot, they have inexpensive rooms to rent upstairs as well.

Bacchus/Vakhos €€€ *Main beach, Mesongí, tel: 26610 7530.* This idyllically set beachfront taverna, going for over four decades, prides itself on sourcing local, fresh seafood like *góno* (baby) *kalamári*, large prawns from the Amvrakikós Gulf, perfectly fried *koutsomoúra* and naturally coloured *taramosaláta*; farmed northern Greek mussels are an exception. Fresh springtime artichokes are fricasseed in white sauce with parsley and celery.

Boukari Beach €€ *Boúkari, 4km (2.5 miles) beyond Mesongí, 600m before the jetty, tel: 26620 51791, www.boukaribeach.gr.* Open lunch and dinner, Easter–Oct. The best of the seafood tavernas at this seashore hamlet, in an idyllic setting with spectacular views of Corfu's east coast. Typical offerings include steamed mussels as a starter, colourful salads, succulent octopus and a range of fresh fish at fair per-kilo prices. The Vlahopoulos family are accomplished hosts, and also have accommodation (see page 137).

Klimataria tou Bellou €€€ *main village square, Benítses, tel: 26610 71201, www.klimataria-restaurant.gr.* Mon–Sat dinner only, Sunday lunch; winter weekends only, but closed 1 Dec–31 Jan. Cult seafood taverna known for purveying only fresh items, and for assiduous service from father-and-son team Nikos and Kostas. Platters include innovative recipes like sardine *bourdéto* or John Dory *biánko*; starters such as leek salad and steamed mussels are commendable too. Good Neméa bulk white wine. Blink and you'll miss the mere seven tables outside (four more inside), so reservations are highly advisable. Save room for Mamma Lily's homemade desserts such as berry-topped cheesecake.

Tripas €€€ *Kynopiástes, 7km (4.5 miles) southwest of Kérkyra, tel: 26610 56333, https://tripas.gr.* Daily May–Oct supper only; otherwise Fri/Sat night only until 11pm. Classic, if rather touristy, taverna where the set-price table d'hôte menu allows a fair sampling of Corfiot dishes (*pastitsáda*, sausage, *stifádo*, *sofríto*) along with some inappropriate dishes like shrimp cocktail, accompanied by very good house red and white wine. The small winter dining room, originally opened as a grocery shop in 1936, is dominated by old bottles, gourds and photos of past celebrity clients. During summer, there's folk dancing out by the courtyard seating.

NORTH OF KÉRKYRA TOWN

Etrusco €€€€ *Káto Korakiána village, on the road down to Dassiá, tel: 26610 93342, www.etrusco.gr.* Apr–Oct, daily 8pm–midnight. Top-calibre nouvelle Italian cooking by father, son and spouses, served in a carefully restored country manor. Specialities like pappardelle with duck and truffles, octopus carpaccio, lamb baked with garlic and kumquat sauce and a 200-label wine list don't come cheap, but this has been ranked as one of the best five Greek tavernas outside of Athens. Advance reservations required.

Roula's €€ *Kondókali, well signposted on the Nisí Gerékou peninsula, tel: 26610 91832, http://taverna-roula.gr. Summer daily lunch and dinner, winter dinner Mon–Sat, Sun lunch.* A favourite venue for a seafood meal, especially out on the terrace overlooking the marina. Scaly fish like *sykiós* (corb) or *mylokópi* (ombrine) is well priced and grilled to perfection; ask for it *petáli* style (butterflied). Starter portions are decent, though opt for beer, bottled wine or ouzo rather than their average bulk wine.

THE NORTHEAST

Cavo Barbaro (Tou Foti) €€€ *Avláki mid-beach, east of Kassiópi, tel: 26630 81905. Daily all day May–Oct.* A competent beach taverna, with welcoming service. Starters might encompass beet salad with yogurt and walnuts, aubergine soufflé, and *plevrótous*; mains may include *sofríto*, baked lamb and seafood like octopus carpaccio or scaly fish. For dessert, try the chocolate soufflé with vanilla ice cream. There's seating on the lawn, or on flagstones under a pergola, and plenty of parking. The only thing 'barbarous' here can be the wind, as there's no shelter; check direction and strength before heading downhill.

Filaraki € *Main road, Aharávi, south (inland) side, about halfway along the 'strip', tel: 26630 64750. Daily most of the year noon–1.30am.* Carnivore heaven, and about the only place in Aharávi where locals dine. After midnight, other taverna-keepers who've closed for the evening come here – a telling endorsement. Principal main dishes are succulent *kondosoúvli* (spit-roasted pork chunks) and *arní soúvlas* (spit-roasted lamb chunks), while starters include excellent *tyrokafterí* (spicy cheese dip), salads and spicy grilled *plevrótous* (oyster mushrooms). Corfu draught beer or homemade bulk wine to drink. A pleasant interior for cooler months; otherwise dine on the terrace.

Glyfa €€€ *between Glýfa beach and main road, between Barbáti and Nissáki, tel: 26630 91090, https://tavernaglyfa.com. Apr–Oct, lunch and dinner (until midnight), reservations suggested.* The 'It' seafood taverna along this stretch of shoreline; parking is difficult so many diners arrive by boat (the restaurant can organise this). Expect assiduous service, proper table linen, a well-priced premium-Greek wine list, king scallops as an appetiser, great seafood mains, and a few meat dishes for the fish-averse. Desserts might include pavlova, chocolate soufflé or panna cotta.

Kouloura €€€ *Kouloúra cove, tel: 26630 91253,* www.tavernakouloura. com. Easter–early Oct daily 11am–9pm, early evening closure means this isn't a good bet for dinner. For 'Kensington-on-Sea', moderately priced seafood, a large selection of *mezédes*, plus unusually elaborate *píttes* (baked pies) and pulse dishes at this impeccably set taverna overlooking one of Corfu's most photogenic anchorages. Reservations needed in peak season.

Nikolas €€ *Agní cove south end, tel: 26630 91243,* www.agnibay.com. Daily May–Oct lunch and dinner. This taverna is the oldest one here, built as a family home and café in 1892. Today, Perikles and his family serve Corfiot specialities like aubergine-and-cheese bourékia and lamb kapamá, plus grilled sardines, along with their own wines (the bulk red is excellent). Tear yourself away from the picturesque view to browse the old photos and maps lining the walls inside. Dinner reservations needed during peak season, especially for Thursday 'Greek nights'.

Tavernaki €€ *Kassiópi port, far end east shore, tel: 26630 81529.* Daily Apr–Oct lunch and dinner, winter weekends only. Portions are medium-sized to large, so appear hungry – salads suffice for two. Corfu beer on draught (500ml) is featured at a keen price; there's also good bulk rosé wine. Summer wood-deck seating has impeccable views to the port and lit-up castle; in cooler weather a glass windbreak goes up to create a 'greenhouse', while winter tables are inside. Good service; do book in peak season.

The Old School € *Kassiópi main port roundabout, tel: 26630 81211.* May–Oct lunch (until 4pm) & dinner (until late). A favourite venue for seafood and generous meat casseroles including pork or lamb kótsi (shank). If possible, sit beneath their giant plane tree. Local microbrewery products are featured (normally priced), plus Belgian beers (expensive) and *hýma* wine (the local rosé is fine and dry).

Toula €€€ *Agní cove, tel: 26630 91350*, www.toulasagni.com. May–Oct daily lunch and dinner, 1–11pm. Worth special mention for its professional demeanour, nice line in hot mezédes and their famous *garídes Toula* – grilled prawns with spicy mixed-rice pilaf. Any seafood main dish, washed down by excellent bulk white wine, is a likely winner.

THE NORTH AND NORTHWEST

Akrogiali €€ *Far south end of the bay, Ágios Geórgios Págon, tel: 6946 027742*. 15 May–6 Oct daily. A bumpy, wash-out-prone track leads 1,500m (1,640yds) south from the beach to this little eyrie (marked by a windmill). Per-kilo fish prices are fair for Corfu, and *mezédes* include appealing oddities like carrot salad and fish croquettes. The lowest terrace is lapped by the sea.

Foros € *Paleá Períthia, tel: 6980 265348*. May–Oct daily, otherwise weekends only. One of the first tavernas in this once-deserted Venetian village, working out of a former café on the original square, and still one of the best – Rick Stein has called in approvingly. The emphasis here is on grills, but you can have a very enjoyable *mezédes*-only meal – sausages, *kremydópita* (onion turnover), and stuffed peppers – while downing *tsípouro* or bulk wine. Finish off with their famous *karydópita* (walnut cake) and ice cream.

Kohili €€€ *Ágios Stéfanos Gýrou, tel: 26630 51629*, www.delfinoblu.gr. May–Oct dinner only. For a romantic evening, book a table amid wicker chairs and gauzy curtains at the gourmet diner of recommended Delfino Blu Hotel. From the veranda tables you'll have a stupendous view across the ocean into the sunset. The fare is generic Mediterranean, encompassing risotto, pasta, salads and some Greek platters, complemented by fine wines from proprietor Kostas' mainland home region of Kalambáka. Very polished service.

Panorama €€ *Afiónas village centre, above Afiónas beach, tel: 26630 51846*. From Afiónas beach (the far northwest end of Ágios Geórgios Págon bay), this taverna is just a hop and a jump up by car. This place lives up to its name with eyefuls of Graviá, Mathráki and Othoní islets.

Order anything from snack plates to courgette fritters, smoked mackarel and draught beers.

THE WEST

Antonis € *Pélekas, tel: 26610 94289.* Open daily noon until late much of the year. The best value of several tavernas here for grills, *mezédes* and salads. They also have the calmest outdoor terrace in what can be a rather traffic-plagued village.

Elizabeth's € *Doukádes village centre, tel: 26630 41728.* Open daily for lunch and dinner most of the year. Elizabeth's has been going since the 1940s, and is now in the hands of the founder's granddaughter. Reliable dishes include cockerel pastitsáda with extra-fat noodles, and peas with potatoes. The purplish bulk wine is rough and ready, as is the *objet trouvé* decor (ancient bottles and a jukebox that has sadly expired). For once, a place that's definitely more fun to eat at inside than out. Cash only.

ERÍKOUSA

Acantha €€€ *north end main beach, tel: 6945 227196,* https://acanthahotel.com. Restaurant of the eponymous boutique hotel, run by Franca and Sandro who retired here after a life spent travelling the globe. The food, especially fish and desserts, is the best on this islet – well worth the outlay, accompanied by top-drawer Tuscan wine.

PAXÍ

Paxoimadi € *Lákka, just in from quay, tel: 26620 33098.* An excellent choice for lunch. Try tasty platters of lentil salad and grape-leaf *dolmádes* or traditional mains of moussakás, kalamári, or marídes.

A–Z TRAVEL TIPS

A SUMMARY OF PRACTICAL INFORMATION

A

ACCOMMODATION

Hotels. Many hotels are heavily booked with package tours in summer, especially between early July and early September, so advance reservations are strongly recommended. Recourse to the usual third-party booking websites can be successful; in slow years package operators have online specials.

Hotels are rated from 1-star to 5-star, based more on their common areas and amenities than the actual rooms. Prices can vary widely within each category, while luxury (5-star) establishments are not price controlled. Thus, a 3-star hotel room may be just as comfortable as a 5-star room, but common areas will not include a conference room, hairdresser, gym, spa.or multiple restaurants. All hotels of 2-star rating and above are reasonably furnished, have en-suite rooms and should provide breakfast.

Villas and apartments. Corfu has more villas, multi-bedroom apartments and studios than many other Greek tourist centres. Accommodation ranges from simple flats to lavishly appointed summer homes –sometimes tastefully converted from a traditional house or building– complete with swimming pools. In the UK, several companies specialise in secluded luxury villas on both Corfu and Paxí: Sunvil (www.sunvil.co.uk), Greek Islands Club (www.gicthevillacollection.com), Simpson Travel (www.simpsontravel.com) and Travel à la Carte (www.travelalacarte.co.uk). More affordable are Oliver's Travels (oliverstravels.com) and TUI Villas with Pools (www.tui.co.uk).

I'd like a single/double room **Tha íthela éna monóklino/díklino**
How much do you charge? **Póso hreónete?**

AIRPORT

Located about 4km (2.2 miles) from the capital, Corfu's lagoon-side airport (CFU) is capable of handling all but the largest jets. This antiquated terminal has long had a poor reputation; however, it is one of 14 Greek regional airports acquired by the German entity Fraport, who in the coming years should build state-of-the art arrival and departure facilities.

Delayed departures (and arrivals) are depressingly common. In case of a really long, confirmed delay in take-off, it's better to walk 700m/yds to the shore of Garítsa Bay where proper cafés and tavernas await.

The currency-exchange office opens from 9am until 2am if there are international flights scheduled to land late at night. (It's a good idea to arrive with a few euros in hand, in case the airport office is closed, though there is at least one ATM in the airport.)

Bus No. 15 (Blue Bus) links the airport with Sarokko Square in Kérkyra Town. It runs daily between 7.30am–11pm, continuing to the new port until 10pm. For details and current timetables go to www.astikok telkerkyras.gr. Taxis charge an inflated €12–15 for the short run into town. Pre-booked car rental is so advantageously priced that there's little point in submitting to their tender mercies.

You can track flight arrivals and departures at www.europe-airports. com.

B

BICYCLE AND SCOOTER HIRE

You can hire bicycles and scooters in all the tourist centres. However, many package operators warn clients against scooters for legitimate fear of an accident (and to drum up more business for organised excursions). It is vital that you check that scooter/motorbike use does not invalidate your holiday insurance.

To hire a motorbike with an engine of 50–125cc displacement you must be at least 18 years old and hold a driving license authorised for Class A (look on the back of a UK one). American licenses must include Class M1. Rental agencies have become quite strict on this point – zealous police are fining both them and riders up to €1,000 for violations. It is also illegal to ride without a crash helmet – the fines issued at checkpoints are similarly draconian.

It is certainly not advisable to ride a motorbike in a swimsuit, since burns or scrapes resulting from even a slight accident could be appalling. Inspect brakes and tyres before hiring, and drive with care. Even on notionally good roads there are occasional potholes or treacherous gravel patches.

Bicycle hire is less common because of Corfu's mountainous terrain, but a good place for serious bikers is the Corfu Mountain Bike Shop (tel: 26610 93344; www.mountainbikecorfu.gr), on the main road at Dassiá. It organises expeditions on Giant bicycles.

BUDGETING FOR YOUR TRIP

Corfu is not the cheapest of the Greek islands, and probably as costly as most other Mediterranean destinations. In high season, the rate for a good 4-star hotel is around €180 minimum per night for a double room. Booking an airfare/accommodation package will yield a substantial saving.

A three-course meal plus drinks in a decent restaurant or taverna costs around €20–30 per person. Car hire for a compact ranges from about €20 per day (low season) up to €50 per day in peak season, if pre-booked online. Public transport and museum fees are inexpensive.

C

CAR HIRE

It is definitely worth hiring a car in order to explore Corfu. As elsewhere in Greece, this is not particularly cheap in peak season, but it is certainly less expensive than touring by taxi, and less frustrating than coping with irregular public transport. For a decent family-sized car in high season, budget €550 minimum per week, and choose a model with air conditioning.

In high season, advance online reservation is essential. Some of the best consolidator websites include www.auto-europe.co.uk, www.car rentals.co.uk and www.rentalcargroup.com. A local outfit on Corfu giving uniformly good, hassle-free service is AutoUnion, just outside the airport (tel: 26610 33977).

Those intending to hire a car should carry an International Driving Permit if from the US, Canada or Australia (national licences alone are not valid and heavy fines ensue if you're detected driving without an IDP). Alternatively all European Economic Area national driving licences are accepted, provided that they have been held for one full year and the driver is over 21 years of age (sometimes 23 years for certain agencies). After Brexit this may change for UK licence holders. You will also need a credit card for a damages deposit.

Many brochure rates seem attractive because they do not include personal insurance, collision damage waiver (CDW) or VAT at 24 percent. Most agencies have a waiver excess of between €400 and €700 – the amount (pre-blocked on your credit card) you're responsible for if your vehicle gets smashed or stolen, even with CDW coverage. It is strongly suggested you purchase extra cover (often called Super CDW or Liability Waiver Surcharge) to reduce this risk to zero; UK or North American residents can buy good-value annual policies from entities like Insurance4CarHire (www.insurance4carhire.com) or Voyager (www.voyageroasis.co.uk). Policies sold on the spot are invariably ripoffs.

I'd like to hire a car (tomorrow) **Tha íthela na nikiáso éna avtokínito (ávrio)**
What's the hire charge per day? **Póso kostízi tin iméra?**

CLIMATE

July and August are the sunniest, hottest and busiest tourist months. You may prefer to stay between mid-May and late June or from early September to mid-October. At any time outside mid-June to August it might rain, but global climate change has disrupted long-established weather patterns.

In winter it rains very hard. November through February are the wettest months and January the coldest, but even during mid-winter, frost is rare except at altitude. Spring, when Corfu bursts with wild flowers, is the best time for walking.

The chart shows each month's average air and sea temperature in Celsius and Fahrenheit, and the average number of hours of sunshine per day.

	J	F	M	A	M	J	J	A	S	O	N	D
Air												
°C	10	10	12	15	19	24	27	26	23	19	15	12
°F	50	50	54	59	66	75	81	79	73	66	59	54
Sea												
°C	15	15	15	16	18	21	24	25	24	21	19	18
°F	59	59	59	61	64	70	75	77	75	70	66	64
Sunshine hours												
	5	6	7	7	9	10	11	12	9	6	4	3

CLOTHING

Clothing is almost always casual on Corfu, though multistar hotels enforce a dress code at dinnertime. It is also appropriate to dress up a little for a night in Kérkyra Town. Choose lightweight cotton clothes in spring and summer, and a warm jacket, sweater and rainwear in autumn or winter. A pocket umbrella is a good idea in any season except mid-summer.

CRIME AND SAFETY (see also Emergencies and Police)

The Corfiots, like most Greeks, are scrupulously honest. However, of late, organised burglary rings are targeting foreign-owned or tenanted villas in the north of the island, so take appropriate precautions. Those staying in a hotel should use the room safe rather than circulate with excess valuables. Car break-ins (especially at isolated beach parking areas) are becoming more common. Take a photocopy of your passport, rather than the original, out with you (you're required to have official ID on your person at all times in Greece).

Possession of recreational drugs is a serious matter in Greece, though medical cannabis is now permitted. Keep prescription drugs in their original containers, and keep documentation handy for insulin syringes.

Huge, jointed red-and-yellow wasps are a mid-summer hazard, especially around swimming pools. Their sting is excruciating; Fenistil gel (from any pharmacy) dulls the pain.

D

DRIVING

Road conditions. Main roads are generally very good, but secondary roads are some of the narrowest and most treacherous on any of the Greek islands. Curves are often indicated too late, sometimes un-signposted and rarely banked correctly. If there is a mirror on a bend, brake and down-shift – it is probably going to be extremely tight or narrow, or perhaps both. Rockslides are common during the rainy season, and broken shoulders or potholes are not unknown on even the best-paved stretches; anything marked 'unsurfaced' on a map can be very rough indeed. Drive with extreme caution, as you are responsible for damage sustained to the underside of your hire car, even with comprehensive coverage.

Other drivers are a major hazard. Greeks love to straddle the median line, barge out recklessly from side-roads, or overtake on either side. One-way street systems are often regarded, especially by two-wheelers, as optional.

Rules and regulations. Drive on the right side and overtake (theoretically) on the left. Roundabouts and traffic lights are eccentrically arranged by north-European standards. If an oncoming driver flashes the lights, it means 'Stay where you are, I'm coming through', not 'Go ahead'. It can also mean 'traffic control ahead'. Seat belts are obligatory, as is the carrying of your driving licence for anyone driving. Speed limits are 50kph (30mph) inside built-up areas, 90/110kph (56/68mph) on ordinary roads. In practice, however, Corfu's winding roads usually set the speed limit – it's difficult to safely exceed 50kph (30mph).

Fuel. Unless you are on the top of Mt Pandokrátor, you will never be far from a filling station. However, in rural areas they are open only until about 8pm and close on Sunday. On busy main roads and in resorts they open daily from early until late. A few big filling stations have after-hours automatic-sales pumps, using euro notes.

If you need help. Your car hire office should provide contact numbers for breakdown service. If you are involved in an accident with another vehicle and/or with significant personal injury or property damage, it is illegal to leave the scene – wait for the ordinary police or traffic police (*trohéa*) to show up and take statements.

Corfu roads readily generate punctures – unfortunately, tyre-repair shops are concentrated in the middle of the island, around Gouviá. A good one there is Pangratis, on the northeast side of the highway (tel: 26610 91495).

Road signs. On main roads these are in Greek and Latin (Western) letters; on secondary roads they may just be in Greek. Critical junctions are atrociously indicated, with vital signs sometimes either uprooted or hidden by foliage.

Detour **ΠΑΡΑΚΑΨΗ**/Parákampsi
Parking **ΠΑΡΚΙΓΚ**/Párking
Forbidden **...ΑΠΑΓΟΡΕΥΕΤΑΙ**/...apagorévete
Be careful **ΠΡΟΣΟΧΗ**/Prosohí
Bus stop **ΣΤΑΣΗ ΛΕΟΦΟΡΙΟΥ**/Stasí leoforíou
Stop **ΣΤΑΜΑΤΑ**/Stamáta
For pedestrians **ΓΙΑ ΠΕΖΟΥΣ**/Gia pezoús
Danger **ΚΙΝΔΙΝΟΣ**/Kíndinos
No entry **ΑΠΑΓΟΡΕΥΕΤΑΙ Η ΕΙΣΟΔΟΣ**/Apagorévete i ísodos

E

ELECTRICITY

Corfu has 220-volt/50-cycle AC current out of European Type F (earthed, heavy duty appliance) or Type C (unearthed). Sockets take two round-pin plugs, so bring an adapter or transformer with you as necessary.

EMBASSIES AND CONSULATES

There are consular offices for the UK and the Republic of Ireland in Kérkyra Town. Embassies of main countries are located in Athens.

Australian Embassy and Consulate Level 6, Thon Building, junction Kifisías & Alexándras, 115 21 Athens, tel: 210 87 04 000, http://greece.embassy.gov.au/athn/home.html.

British Vice Consulate: Mantzárou 18, Kérkyra Town, tel: 26610 23457 (in practice calls are forwarded to an Athens voice-mail), www.gov.uk/world/organisations/british-vice-consulate-corfu. Open Mon–Fri 9am–1pm for emergencies.

British Embassy: Ploutárhou 1, 106 75 Athens, tel: 210 72 72 600, www.gov.uk/world/organisations/british-embassy-athens.

Canadian Embassy: 48 Ethnikis Antistaseos Street, Chalandri, 152 31 Athens, tel: 210 72 73 400.

Irish Honorary Consulate: 20A Kapodistríou Street, Kérkyra Town, tel: 26610 33411.

Irish Embassy: Vassiléos Konstandínou 7, 106 74 Athens, tel: 210 72 32 771/2, www.dfa.ie/irish-embassy/greece.

South African Embassy and Consulate: Kifisías 60, 151 25 Marousi, Athens, tel: 210 61 06 645.

US Embassy and Consulate: Vassilísis Sofías 91, 101 60 Athens, tel: 210 72 12 951, https://gr.usembassy.gov.

EMERGENCIES

Police, tel: **100**.
Ambulance, tel: **166**.

Fire, tel: **199**.

ENVIRONMENTAL ISSUES

Many visitors are shocked by overflowing wheelie bins across the island. Rubbish is rarely collected because the old landfill near Temblóni is full, and not up to EU standards. The siting of a new, legal landfill is the hot local issue, with no resolution in sight. Lefkímmi was approached, but declined the 'honour' with a massive civil disobedience campaign. Garbage mountains will likely remain a feature of the landscape for some time to come.

G

GETTING THERE

It is possible to cross Europe overland and take a ferry to Corfu from Venice, Ancona, Brindisi or Bari in Italy. However, for most visitors, air travel (around 3 hours' flight time from Britain) is the only practical route. Charter or no-frills flights from the UK link a dozen British airports to Corfu; BA, Jet2, easyJet, TUI, and Ryanair provide seasonal scheduled services from several UK airports. If you are travelling from North America, fly to London or another major European hub and pick up a cheap flight from there.

H

HEALTH AND MEDICAL CARE

Doctors and dentists are concentrated in Kérkyra Town; your hotel or apartment owner will be able to find you one who speaks English. Most resorts have a public medical clinic.

The capital's hospital and general clinic operate a 24-hour emergency service that dispatches ambulances to any point on the island with admirable speed. The Corfu General Hospital (tel: 26613 60400) is 4km (2 miles) out of Kérkyra Town, in Kondókali. Privately run Corfu General Clinic (www.

corfugeneralclinic.gr) is located on the main Paleokastrítsa road, just outside Kérkyra Town centre (tel: 26610 36044 or 26610 22946). Emergency
treatment in public facilities is free, although this only covers immediate
needs. EU residents can get free treatment with a European Health Insurance Card (EHIC; www.ehic.org.uk). It is advisable to have travel insurance
to cover you for protracted treatment or repatriation.

A green cross on a white background identifies a chemist (pharmacy)
– *farmakío* (ΦΑΡΜΑΚΕΙΟ). They are normally open only 9am–2pm Monday to Friday, but a notice on the door specifies the nearest one for
after-hours/weekend service.

a doctor/dentist **énas giatrós/odontogiatrós**
hospital **nosokomío**
an upset stomach **anakatoméno stomáhi**
sunstroke **ilíasi**
a fever **pyretós**

L

LANGUAGE

Only in remote countryside spots will non-Greek-speaking tourists run
into serious communication problems. You will find that basic English
is spoken almost everywhere, as are Italian, German and French, to
some degree.

Stress is a very important feature of the Greek language, denoted by
an accent above the vowel of the syllable to be emphasised. We have indicated proper stress in all of our transliterations of multi-syllable words.

The table given lists the Greek letters in their upper- and lower-case
forms, followed by the closest individual or combined letters to which
they correspond in the English language, and a pronunciation guide.
Do not be alarmed if you encounter other transliterations on Corfu

A	α	a	as in *father*
B	β	v	as in veto
Γ	γ	g	as in *go* (except before *i* and *e* sounds, when it's like the *y* in *yes*)
Δ	δ	d	sounds like *th* in *then*
E	ε	e	as in *get*
Z	ζ	z	same as in English
H	η	i	as in *ski*
Θ	θ	th	as in *thin*
I	ι	i	as in *ski*
K	κ	k	same as in English
Λ	λ	l	same as in English
M	μ	m	same as in English
N	ν	n	same as in English
Ξ	ξ	x	as in *box*
O	o	o	as in *road*
Π	π	p	same as in English
P	ρ	r	same as in English
Σ	σ, ς	s	as in *kiss*, except like *z* before *m* or *g* sounds
T	τ	t	same as in English
Y	υ	y	as in *country*
Φ	φ	f	same as in English
X	χ	h	rough, as in Scottish *loch*
Ψ	ψ	ps	as in *tipsy*
Ω	ω	o	as in *long*
AI	αι	e	as in *hay*
AY	αυ	av	as in *avant-garde*
EI	ει	i	as in *ski*
EY	ευ	ev	as in *ever*
OI	οι	i	as in *ski*

ΟΥ	ou	ou	as in *soup*
ΓΓ	γγ	ng	as in *longer*
ΓΚ	γκ	g	as in *gone*
ΓΞ	γξ	nx	as in *anxious*
ΜΠ	μπ	b or mb	as in *beg* or *compass*
ΝΤ	ντ	d or nd	as in *dog* or *under*

– several schemes exist. For example, the word *ágios* is often also spelled *ághios* and *áyios* in the Roman alphabet, although it is always pronounced the same.

LGBTQ TRAVELLERS

Corfu has no specific gay scene, but attitudes in resorts are generally relaxed. Be discreet in conservative rural communities. Homosexual practice is legal in Greece for people aged 17 and older.

M

MAPS

The folding Kérkyra Town plan handed out by the tourist-info kiosk on Platía Sarókko is the best available. For a commercial touring map of the entire island, plump for Anavasi Edition's 1:40,000 folding map of the entire island – preferably bought before arrival, though often Plous Books at Nikifórou Theotóki 91 in Kérkyra Town stocks it.

MEDIA

Newspapers: In season, major English newspapers can be bought in resorts one day after publication. Some English tabloids have European editions printed in Greece and available the same day. Greek news in English can be found at www.ekathimerini.com and https://greece.greekreporter.com/category/greek-news.

Television: Most large hotels have satellite TV services, which include news channels such as CNN and BBC World. Greek TV stations often broadcast American and English films and other imported programmes in the original language, with Greek subtitles.

MONEY

Currency: Greece's currency is the euro (€). Notes are denominated in 5, 10, 20, 50, 100 and 200 euros; coins in 1 and 2 euros and 1, 2, 5, 10, 20 and 50 cents, known as *leptá* in Greece. Notes of 100 euros and above are regarded with suspicion, as possibly counterfeit, and can often only be exchanged in banks. 500-euro notes were withdrawn from circulation in 2018 because of their popularity with mega-criminals.

Currency exchange: Most banks exchange foreign currency but charge a commission (usually 1–3 percent) for the service. Exchange rates appear on a digital display, and are identical for each bank.

The best option for exchanging foreign notes is the Bank of Greece (not to be confused with the National Bank of Greece) at Dimárhou Kollá 1, just off Platía Dimarhíou. Rates are good and commissions low to nonexistent.

ATMs: There are cash machines in every Corfiot town or resort of over a few hundred inhabitants. These are the most convenient way to get euros.

Credit and debit cards: As part of the Greek government's campaign to stamp out the thriving black economy, card transactions are actively encouraged at hotels, tavernas, supermarkets and filling stations. Surprisingly unlikely-looking enterprises have the

I want to change some pounds/dollars **Thélo na alláxo merikés líres/meriká dollária**
Can I pay with this credit card? **Boró na pliróso me aftí tin pistotikí kárta?**

necessary device.

Travellers cheques: These are not recommended for use in Greece – expect severe delays or outright refusals in banks.

O

OPENING TIMES

Opening times vary between official organisations and privately owned shops and cafés, and also from high to low season. Almost everybody closes mid-afternoon, and official entities will not reopen later; if you need to get anything official done, do so in the morning.

We give opening days and hours for museums and archaeological sites in the text, but remember that the last admission ticket is generally sold 20 minutes before closing time. Shops are open Monday, Wednesday and Saturday 9am–2.30pm, closing at 2pm on Tuesday, Thursday and Friday, but open additionally 5.30–8.30pm on those days. In peak season, they may stay open throughout the day until midnight, especially if selling tourist-related products. Supermarkets open 8.30am–9pm Mon–Fri, 8.30am–8pm Sat; a very few may work 10am–4pm Sunday. Restaurants and tavernas do lunch from just after noon until 3.45pm, and begin dinner service at around 6.30pm, but most Greek families don't eat until after 9pm. Banks are open Mon–Fri 8am–2pm.

P

POLICE (see Emergencies)

Regular police officers wear two-toned blue uniforms. Tourist police also wear blue uniforms displaying a small national flag indicating which language they speak other than Greek.

If you need to report an incident to the police, go to the police station closest to the scene of the crime. Each group of villages has a designated police station.

> Where's the nearest police station? **Pou íne to kondinótero astynomikó tmíma?**

Traffic police check car documents and driving licences, operate speed and drink-driving traps and issue hefty fines for illegal parking. Car hire companies will use your credit card details to pay ignored parking tickets; you have 10 working days to pay moving violations in person. Failing that, a court date will be set, and a summons sent to your home address. Failure to appear will result in an extra conviction for contempt of court, and make re-entry to Greece extremely awkward.

POST OFFICES

Post offices have blue-and-yellow livery, and are marked 'Elliniká Takhydromía' in Greek plus 'Hellenic Post' in English, with a stylised Hermes head as the logo. Stamps can be bought here, or at postal agencies (usually small shops).

Post offices are generally open Mon–Fri 7.30am–2pm. The main Kérkyra Town post office at the corner of Alexándhras 26 and Zafiropoúlou is open Mon–Fri 7.30am–8.30pm (until 2.30pm for money orders and parcels). Registered letters and parcels to non-EU destinations are examined before being sent, so don't seal them beforehand.

Mailboxes are yellow with the same Hermes-head logo, but in rural areas they are not emptied regularly. Most hotels will post letters and postcards for you. Allow 4–7 days for postcards to Europe, 9–14 days for the rest of the world.

PUBLIC HOLIDAYS

Banks, offices and shops are closed on the following national holidays,

> A stamp for this letter/postcard **Éna grammatósimo giavtó to grámma/giavtí tin kart postál**

as well as during some local festivals:

1 January *Protohroniá* New Year's Day
6 January *Theofánia* Epiphany
25 March *Evangelismós Day* Greek Independence/Annunciation
1 May May Day
15 August *Kímisi tis Theotókou* Dormition of the Mother of God
28 October *Ohi* ('No') Day, celebrates 1940 defiance of Italians
25 December *Hristoúgena* Christmas
26 December *Sýnaxis tis Panagías* Gathering of the Virgin's Entourage

Moveable religious festivals:
The first day of Lent (*Kathari Deftéra*/Clean Monday), Good Friday, Easter Monday and *tou Agíou Pnévmatos*/Whit Monday.

R

RELIGION

Corfu, like the rest of Greece, is largely Greek Orthodox in faith. There is, however, a sizeable but well-integrated Catholic minority with a handful of functioning churches in Kérkyra Town. The Holy Trinity Anglican Church at Lorénzou Mavíli 21 (www.holytrinitycorfu.net), in the Pórta Remoúnda district of Kérkyra Town, holds weekly services – visitors are welcome.

You must dress modestly to visit churches or monasteries, which normally means long trousers for men, a long skirt for women and covered shoulders for both sexes. Men might be allowed to wear long shorts which cover knees, and wraps are sometimes provided for under-dressed women.

T

TELEPHONES

Since deregulation of the local telecoms market, a number of providers offer competition to the state-run OTE. OTE still, however, maintains most of the increasingly scarce public booths. Kiosks and newsagents sell OTE calling cards in various unit denominations, as well as other products (including discount long-distance cards and local mobile top-up cards).

Most hotels of two stars and above have direct-dial lines out, but add a huge surcharge to the cost of calls. Avoid this by using a pre-paid, 12-digit code card with an access number.

Dialling from abroad, the country code for Greece is 30. Within Greece, all phone numbers have ten digits; fixed lines begin with 2, mobiles with 69. There are no longer any area codes as such in Greece – what were the old codes are now merely the prefixes: 26610 for Kérkyra Town and the centre of the island, 26630 for northern Corfu, 26620 for the far south and Paxí.

Foreign visitors with tri-band mobiles can roam on one of the Greek networks, but charges for non-EU subscribers are extortionate. If you are staying more than a week or two, and also planning to return to Greece, it makes sense for them to buy a local SIM with some talk-time included. It (and your device) must be registered at time of purchase, but the number remains valid for some months from each top-up. On the northeast coast, do not let your phone be 'snatched' by an Albanian network opposite; if you do you will have an unpleasant non-EU-roaming-bill back home.

TIME ZONES

Greek time is GMT + 2. Greece observes Daylight Savings along with the rest of Europe (but not the USA), moving clocks one hour forward between the last Sunday in March and the last one in October. However, the European Parliament has voted to end Daylight Savings in 2021. It is unclear whether this will happen, or whether the UK will go along with this post Brexit.

In August, here is the time in the following cities:

New York	London	Jo'burg	**Corfu**	Sydney	Auckland
5am	10am	11am	**noon**	8pm	9pm

TOILETS

Public conveniences are best avoided. But if you are desperate in Kérkyra Town, there are toilets at the following locations: Platía I. Theotóki, near the Spianáda bandstand, on Platía Sarókko and at Platía Spiliás near the old port. Take along your own toilet paper. You should leave a small tip (up to €0.50) if there's someone in attendance.

You are always expected to put toilet tissue in the waste bin rather than down the toilet. Due to their narrow-bore drainage pipes, older toilets easily become clogged.

TOURIST INFORMATION

The Greek National Tourist Organisation, or Ellinikós Organismós Tourismoú (EOT; www.visitgreece.gr) has the following offices abroad, fine for general info and glossy pamphlets, but short on material specific to Corfu:

UK and Ireland: 5th Floor East, Great Portland House, 4 great Portland Street, London W1W 8QJ; tel: (020) 7495 9300.

US: 800 Third Avenue, 23rd Floor, New York, NY 10022; tel: (212) 421 5777.

The tourist information office in Kérkyra Town is a small, green, wooden kiosk halfway up the Ioánni Theotókou side of Platía Sarókko (unreliable opening hours in season) – though information is limited to a useful town plan and basic leaflets.

TRANSPORT

Buses *(leoforía)*. The island's public bus service is not always efficient, but it is good value. Timetables are displayed at bus stops (ΣΤΑΣΗ– *stási*) in the capital. There are no all-night bus services. There are two types of buses on the island. The blue urban buses serve towns and villages in the vicinity of Kérkyra Town, including Benítses, Kondókali, Gouviá, Dassiá, the Achilleion and Pélekas. Buses for Kanóni depart from near the Spianáda. All other blue buses leave from Platía Saríkko (San Rocco Square) (tel: 26610 31595). Detailed information on routes and timetables can be obtained at www.astikoktelkerkyras.gr. Long-distance buses are green-and-cream-coloured, but with variations for adverts; they leave from the coach station on Avramíou Street by the New Fort (tel: 26610 39985). Check https://greenbuses.gr for routes and timetables.

For all buses, buy your tickets on board or from kiosks in the square. You should only flag buses down at designated stops, or other safe places, with a verge.

Taxis. Taxis based in Kérkyra Town are dark blue; those based in the country are grey. Taxi ranks in town are at the new port, old port, Esplanade and San Rocco Square. There are meter tariffs: check upon getting into the cab; if the meter is mysteriously 'broken', you will have to agree on a fare with the driver.

Ferries. Regular ferries run to the Diapóndia islets from Ágios Stéfanos Gýrou, and to Paxí via Igoumenítsa. But the Ionian islands are not a group for island-hopping: it takes three hours to sail to Paxí and the former service to Kefaloniá has been suspended. To get to either Itháki, Kefalloniá or Zákynthos requires changing on the Greek mainland at Astakós or Pátra. Ferries also go to various ports in Italy. All depart from Kérkyra Town, though there is an additional service to Igoumenítsa from Lefkímmi (near Kávos) – useful for drivers since it's much cheaper and quicker.

For current ferry schedules and fares check with authorised

What's the fare to...? **Póso éhi éna isitírio giá...?**
When's the next bus to...? **Póte févgi to epómeno leoforío giá...?**

travel agents or the port authority (http://corfuport.gr; no English option) tel: 26610 45551.

V

VISAS AND ENTRY REQUIREMENTS

European Union (EU) citizens may stay in Greece up to 3 months (longer stays require a residence permit) as long as they have a valid identity card or passport. Citizens of the US, Canada, Australia and New Zealand can stay for up to 90 days within any 180-day period upon production of a valid passport; no advance visas are needed. South African citizens require a Schengen Visa, applied for in advance at a Greek embassy or consulate. Visa requirements for UK nationals in the event of Brexit are uncertain as of writing.

There are no limits on the amount of hard currency visitors can import or export, though amounts in excess of €10,000, or equivalent, should be declared.

All goods brought into Greece for commercial purposes from within the EU must have duty paid on them. There are no limitations on the amount of duty-paid goods that can be brought into the country.

W

WATER

Tap water is not drinkable on much of the island: water here comes from well bores that may have been tainted by the sea (*glyfó* is Greek for brackish, a word you'll hear a lot). Known potable wells are in the square at Benítses, along the waterfront at Garítsa, and on Platía Políti at the top of Guilford in Kérkyra Town. The few springs high in the hills are usually okay to collect from. Bottled water is affordable and is your best bet to avoid any tummy upsets.

WEBSITES AND INTERNET ACCESS

Internet access is available in almost every beach resort, where almost all tavernas, bars and cafés have Wi-Fi zones. These are invariably password-protected. Low-star hotels or pensions tend to have free networks; luxury resorts may control access with a fee or time-limited subscription.

Many Corfu travel agencies and other commercial enterprises have their own websites, which vary greatly in quality. One of the best, and most heavily used, is www.agni.gr (with lively forums). Other useful sites include:

www.terrakerkyra.gr Good overview site, with history, festivals, destinations.

www.allcorfu.com Most up-to-date information on the island's attractions and its people.

http://thecorfiotmagazine.com/archive.html Back issues of the now-defunct monthly to download.

www.corfuwall.gr Weekly events calendar, plus exhaustive information on cultural and other attractions.

http://corfublues.blogspot.com Excellent blog by local aficionado and scholar Jim Potts.

Y

YOUTH HOSTELS

The enormous Pink Palace at Ágios Górdis is the island's backpacker hostel, hosting multi-national crowds in both doubles and multi-bed rooms. Full information from www.thepinkpalace.com.

RECOMMENDED HOTELS

Most of these hotels appear on generic booking websites, and have their own site (often with web discounts). Most listed hotels accept credit cards, and provide air conditioning, unless otherwise stated; prices are B&B except where noted. Beach-resort hotels only operate from late April/early May to October. Most in Kérkyra Town are open year round.

Dialling from outside Greece, precede hotel numbers with the international country code +30.

€€€€€	over 300 euros
€€€€	200–300 euros
€€€	130–200 euros
€€	75–130 euros
€	below 75 euros

KÉRKYRA TOWN

Arkadion €€ double, **€€€** suite *Kapodistríou 44, Kérkyra Town, tel: 26610 30104*, www.arcadionhotel.com. Central 3-star hotel overlooking the Spianáda, four minutes' walk from most museums. Rooms – side-facing ones a bit quieter – are spacious, with wrought-iron bedsteads, marble and wood furniture and beige floor tiles. Common areas include a tiny mezzanine lounge and equally compact first-floor breakfast salon, as well as a roof terrace that's a prime venue for watching the Easter events. 55 rooms and suites.

Bella Venezia €€ double, **€€€** suite *Napoleóndou Zambéli 4, Kérkyra Town, tel: 26610 46500*, www.bellaveneziahotel.com. Kérkyra Town's worst-kept secret, and enduringly popular, this hotel occupies a converted neo-Classical former girls' school at the edge of Pórta Remoúnda district. The best rooms, with high ceilings and sometimes balconies, are on the first two storeys, though third-floor suites can accommodate four; all have computerised climate control and Coco-

Mat natural-fibre bedding. Breakfast is offered in the back-garden conservatory. Stylish lobby bar and helpful staff complete the picture. 31 units. Open Apr–Oct.

Cavalieri €€€ *Kapodistríou Street 4, Kérkyra Town*, tel: 26610 39041, www. cavalieri-hotel-corfu-town.com. This converted six-storey 17th-century mansion, just off the Spianáda, offers an assortment of standard rooms and galleried family rooms (which can fit three at a pinch), though some are on the small and dark side. Worth a visit by non-guests just to enjoy its roof garden's great views while nursing a drink. 50 rooms.

Corfu Palace Hotel €€€€ *Dimokratías 2, Kérkyra Town*, tel: 26610 39485, www.corfupalace.com. The dowager empress of town hotels, a favourite with conferences and business folk as well as holiday-makers, this 5-star outfit scores for its unbeatable position just 10 minutes' walk from the Listón and willing staff, as much for its accommodation. Large standard rooms have veneer floors, while superior units have better soft furnishings; all units have sea views over Garítsa Bay. Breakfast can be taken on the lawn by the saltwater pool, as can the fare of popular summer-weekend barbecues. There's also an indoor pool (with thalassotherapy on tap) by the small spa. 115 rooms.

Hermes € *Gerasímou Markorá 12–14, Pórto Reále area*, tel: 26610 39268, www.hermes-hotel.gr. The Hermes is the town's best budget option, and accordingly much in demand. Decor over two floors of high-ceilinged rooms is in pleasant taste, with light-hued veneer floors and solid-wood Asian furniture, and there are thoughtful touches such as mini sound systems and double glazing. Common areas are limited to a pleasant breakfast salon. 33 rooms.

Konstantinoupolis €€ *Zavitsiánou 11, Old Port*, tel: 26610 48716, http://konstantinoupolis.corfugreecehotels.com. Renovated building dating from 1862, but still pleasantly old-fashioned, this 2-star hotel has both sea and mountain views from the front balconied rooms, which are large – though bathrooms are small and basic, if brightly tiled. Rooms are reached either by a spiral wooden staircase or antique lift, past the more modern mezzanine breakfast area and lounge. 31 rooms.

THE SOUTH

Bella Vista € *Benítses, south edge of village, 100m inland, 300m from marina, tel: 26610 72087,* https://bellavistahotel.gr. Anthea Pouli and assistants preside over unique, youth-orientated accommodation: 23 double rooms in a main building decorated with murals and canvases donated by art students who have stayed here. Two separate annexes contain 20 studios and one-bed apartments (the latter fitting four). Furnishings are basic but the welcome's warm and continental breakfasts excellent. Despite the name, there are no views. Open Easter–Oct.

Boukari Beach € *hotel,* **€€** *villa units Boúkari, tel: 26620 51791,* www.boukaribeach.gr. Some 700m from the excellent, eponymous waterside restaurant, (see page 107). There are two peaceful, secluded units sleeping up to four in each. Studios and double rooms are available in the larger Hotel Penelope, recently refurbished and upgraded. Generous breakfast is included in rates, and there's a large pool out the back. On-site car hire (www.boukari-cars.com) is bookable as a package with your stay, vehicles can be delivered to the airport.

Domes Miramare €€€€ *Moraïtika shore road, tel: 26614 40500,* www.domesmiramare.com. Newest member of the high-end Greek Domes chain, this hotel takes advantage of its prime site. The present iteration comprises just 113 units scattered across tastefully landscaped grounds. There are 14 categories of rooms, suites and villas, the higher ones with private jacuzzis and small pools. Watersports are available off the pebbly beach and there are three onsite a la carte restaurants.

MarBella €€€€ *hillside above Ágios Ioánnis Peristerón beach, tel: 26610 71183,* www.marbella.gr. 1960s-established resort with two adult pools and fancy spa. Many units, cleverly tiered to ensure privacy, gaze across the straits at the mainland. MarBella is expressly family-friendly, with large family-sized suites, limited-hours crêche, kids' clubs by age group, babysitting service and decent food on all-inclusive plans. Otherwise, there are a half-dozen restaurants on site, and half board is the default rate; breakfast includes a live-cooking counter dishing out pancakes, omelettes and so on. Newly opened in 2019 is the adjacent, adults-only Nido Suite Hotel.

NORTH OF KÉRKYRA TOWN

Casa Lucia € *Sgómbou hamlet, at Km 12 of Kérkyra–Paleokastrítsa road, tel: 26610 91419, www.casa-lucia-corfu.com.* A restored olive mill complex set among lovingly tended gardens with a large pool. Nine self-catering units, ranging from studios to family cottages, all share simple (read 1980s vintage), yet adequate furnishings, and are often occupied by patrons attending the yoga, tai chi or massage workshops held here. Peaceful setting at the very centre of the island makes this an excellent touring base. No on-site restaurant or breakfast. Open year round, Nov–Mar on weekly or monthly basis only.

Corfu Imperial €€€€€ *Komméno, tel: 26610 88400, www.corfu imperial.com.* Set at the tip of a private peninsula with man-made sandy-cove beaches on the sheltered inland side, this luxurious hotel is considered one of the two or three top lodgings on the island – and is often booked out. The self-contained resort has a huge seawater swimming pool, waters ports, a choice of restaurants and bars, a tennis club, spa and gym. Rooms are luxuriously furnished and are either in the main block or in bungalows dotted around the pretty grounds with Italianate gardens and olive trees. 306 rooms, suites and villas.

Kontokali Bay €€€€ *Toúrka Peninsula, Kondókali, tel: 26610 99000, www.kontokalibay.com.* This low-rise bungalow-style resort and spa has most units scattered in clusters through beautiful gardens next to a private sandy beach. Superior standards are like junior suites with their sofas and big balconies looking over the lawn to the water, while the family bungalows have garden views. Bathrooms have butler sinks and proper shower screens and facilities are commensurate with the 5-star rating, including an elevated infinity pool, beachside restaurant, state-of-the-art freestanding spa, tennis courts, water sports at the private port and an imaginative children's

broken σπασμένος
spahz•meh•nohs

broom n σκούπα *skoo•pah*

browse ξεφυλλίζω
kseh•fee•lee•zoh

bruise n μελανιά *meh•lah•niah*

brush n βούρτσα *voor•tsah*; v
βουρτσίζω *voor•tsee•zoh*

build κτίζω *ktee•zoh*

building κτίριο *ktee•ree•oh*

burn n έγκαυμα *eh•gahv•mah*

bus λεωφορείο
leh•oh•foh•ree•oh

bus route διαδρομή λεωφορείων
*THee•ah•THroh•mee
leh•oh•foh•ree•ohn*

bus station σταθμός
λεωφορείων *stahTH•mohs
leh•oh•foh•ree•ohn*

bus stop στάση λεωφορείου
stah•see leh•oh•foh•ree•oo

business class μπίζνες θέση
bee•znehs theh•see

business trip επαγγελματικό
ταξίδι *eh•pah•gehl•mah•tee•
koh tah•ksee•THee*

busy (occupied)
απασχολημένος
ah•pahs•khoh•lee•meh•nohs

but αλλά *ah•lah*

butane gas υγραέριο
eegh•rah•eh•ree•oh

butcher shop κρεοπωλείο
kreh•oh•poh•lee•oh

button κουμπί *koo•bee*

buy αγοράζω *ah•ghoh•rah•zoh*

C

cabaret καμπαρέ *kah•bah•reh*

cabin καμπίνα *kah•bee•nah*

cable car τελεφερίκ
teh•leh•feh•reek

cafe καφετέρια
kah•feh•teh•ree•ah

calendar ημερολόγιο
ee•meh•roh•loh•yee•oh

call collect με χρέωση του
καλούμενου *meh khreh•oh•see
too kah•loo•meh•noo*

call n κλήση *klee•see*; v καλώ
kah•loh

camcorder φορητή
βιντεοκάμερα *foh•ree•tee
vee•deh•oh•kah•meh•rah*

camera φωτογραφική μηχανή
*foh•tohgh•rah•fee•kee
mee•khah•nee*

camera case θήκη μηχανής
thee•kee mee•khah•nees

camera store κατάστημα με
φωτογραφικά είδη *kah•tah•
stee•mah meh foh•tohgh•
rah•fee•kah ee•THee*

camp bed κρεβάτι
εκστρατείας *kreh•vah•tee
ehk•strah•tee•ahs*

camping κάμπινγκ *kah•mpeeng*

camping equipment εξοπλισμός
κάμπιγκ *eh•ksohp•leez•mohs
kah•mpeeng*

campsite χώρος κάμπινγκ
khoh•rohs kah•mpeeng

can opener ανοιχτήρι
ah•neekh•tee•ree

Canada Καναδάς *kah•nah•THahs*

canal κανάλι *kah•nah•lee*

cancel v ακυρώνω
ah•kee•roh•noh

cancer (disease) καρκίνος
kahr•kee•nohs

candle κερί *keh•ree*

canoe κανό *kah•noh*

car αυτοκίνητο
ahf•toh•kee•nee•toh

car park [BE] χώρος στάθμευσης
khoh•rohs stahth•mehf•sees

car rental ενοικίαση αυτοκινήτων
*eh•nee•kee•ah•see
ahf•toh•kee•nee•tohn*

car wash πλύσιμο
αυτοκινήτου *plee•see•moh
ahf•toh•kee•nee•too*

carafe καράφα *kah•rah•fah*

caravan τροχόσπιτο
troh•khohs•pee•toh

cards χαρτιά *khahr•tiah*

carpet (fitted) μοκέτα
moh•keh•tah

carton κουτί *koo•tee*

cash desk [BE] ταμείο
tah•mee•oh

cash n μετρητά *meht•ree•tah*;
v εξαργυρώνω
eh•ksahr•ghee•roh•noh

casino καζίνο *kah•see•noh*

castle κάστρο *kahs•troh*

catch v (bus) παίρνω *pehr•noh*

cathedral καθεδρικός ναός
kah•theh•THree•kohs nah•ohs

cave n σπήλαιο *spee•leh•oh*

CD σι ντι *see dee*

cell phone κινητό *kee•nee•toh*

change n αλλαγή *ah•lah•yee*; v
αλλάζω *ah•lah•zoh*

cheap φτηνός *ftee•nohs*

check n (bank) επιταγή *eh•pee•
tah•yee*; (bill) λογαριασμός
loh•ghahr•yahz•mohs

choose διαλέγω *THiah•leh•ghoh*

clean καθαρός *kah•thah•rohs*

cling film [BE] διαφανή
μεμβράνη *THee•ah•fah•nee
mehm•vrah•nee*

clothing store κατάστημα
ρούχων *kah•tahs•tee•mah
roo•khohn*

cold adj (temperature) κρύος
kree•ohs; n (chill) κρυολόγημα
kree•oh•loh•yee•mah

collapse v καταρρέω
kah•tah•reh•oh

collect v παίρνω *peh•rnoh*

color n χρώμα *khroh•mah*

comb n χτένα *khteh•nah*; v
χτενίζω *khteh•nee•zoh*

come έρχομαι *eh•khoh•meh*

come back v (return) επιστρέφω
eh•pees•treh•foh

commission n (agent fee)
προμήθεια proh•_mee_•thee•ah
company n (business) εταιρία
eh•teh•_ree_•ah; (companionship)
παρέα pah•_reh_•ah
complain παραπονιέμαι
pah•rah•poh•_nieh_•meh
computer υπολογιστής
ee•poh•loh•yee•_stees_
concert συναυλία
see•nahv•_lee_•ah
concert hall αίθουσα συναυλιών
_eh_•thoo•sah see•nahv•lee•_ohn_
conditioner (hair)
γαλάκτωμα για τα μαλλιά
ghah•_lah_•ktoh•mah yah tah
mah•_liah_
condom προφυλακτικό
proh•fee•lah•ktee•_koh_
conference συνέδριο
see•_neh_•THree•oh
confirm επιβεβαιώνω
eh•pee•veh•veh•_oh_•noh
constipation δυσκοιλιότητα
thees•kee•lee•_oh_•tee•tah
Consulate Προξενείο
proh•kseh•_nee_•oh
consult v συμβουλεύομαι
seem•voo•_leh_•voh•meh
contact v επικοινωνώ
eh•pee•kee•noh•_noh_
contact fluid υγρό για φακούς
epah•ghr_oh_ yah fah•_koos_
eh•pah•_fees_
contact lens φακοί επαφής
fah•_kohs_ eh•pah•_fees_
contagious μεταδοτικός
meh•tah•THoh•tee•_kohs_
contain περιέχω
peh•ree•_eh_•khoh
contraceptive pill
αντισυλληπτικό χάπι ahn•dee•
see•leep•tee•_koh_ khah•pee
cook n (chef) μάγειρας
mah•yee•rahs; v μαγειρεύω
mah•yee•_reh_•voh

copper χαλκός khahl•_kohs_
corkscrew τιρμπουσόν
teer•boo•_sohn_
corner γωνία ghoh•_nee_•ah
correct v διορθώνω
THee•ohr•_thoh_•noh
cosmetics καλλυντικά
kah•leen•dee•_kah_
cot [BE] παιδικό κρεβάτι
peh•THee•_koh_ kreh•_vah_•tee
cotton βαμβάκι vahm•_vah_•kee
cough n βήχας vee•khahs; v βήχω
vee•khoh
counter ταμείο tah•_mee_•oh
country (nation) χώρα _khoh_•rah
countryside εξοχή eh•ksoh•_khee_
couple n (pair) ζευγάρι
zehv•_ghah_•ree
courier n (messenger) κούριερ
koo•ree•ehr
court house δικαστήριο
THee•kah•_stee_•ree•oh
cramp n κράμπα _krahm_•bah
credit card πιστωτική κάρτα
pees•toh•tee•_kee_ kahr•tah
crib [cot BE] παιδικό κρεβάτι
peh•THee•_koh_ kreh•_vah_•tee
crown n (dental, royal) κορώνα
koh•_roh_•nah
cruise n κρουαζιέρα
kroo•ahz•_yeh_•rah
crutch n (walking support)
δεκανίκι THeh•kah•_nee_•kee
crystal n κρύσταλλο
kree•stah•loh
cup φλυτζάνι flee•_jah_•nee
cupboard ντουλάπα doo•_lah_•pah
currency νόμισμα _noh_•meez•mah
currency exchange office
γραφείο ανταλλαγής
συναλλάγματος ghrah•_fee_•oh
ahn•dah•lah•_yees_
see•nah•_lagh_•mah•tohs
customs (tolls) τελωνείο
teh•loh•_nee_•oh
customs declaration (tolls)

τελωνειακή δήλωση
teh•loh•nee•ah•_kee_
THee•loh•see
cut n (wound) κόψιμο
koh•psee•moh
cut glass n σκαλιστό γυαλί
skah•lees•_toh_ yah•_lee_
cycle helmet κράνος ποδηλάτη
krah•nohs poh•THee•_lah_•tee
cyclist ποδηλάτης
poh•THee•_lah_•tees
Cypriot adj κυπριακός
keep•ree•ah•_kohs_; (nationality)
Κύπριος _kee_•pree•ohs
Cyprus Κύπρος _kee_•prohs

D

damage n ζημιά zee•_miah_;
v καταστρέφω
kah•tah•_streh_•foh
dance v χορεύω khoh•_reh_•voh
dangerous επικίνδυνος
eh•pee•_keen_•THee•nohs
dark adj (color) σκούρος
skoo•rohs
dawn n ξημερώματα
ksee•meh•_roh_•mah•tah
day trip ημερήσια εκδρομή
ee•meh•_ree_•see•ah
ehk•THroh•_mee_
deaf κουφός koo•_fohs_
decide αποφασίζω
ah•poh•fah•_see_•zoh
deck n κατάστρωμα
kah•_tah_•stroh•mah
deck chair σεζ-λόνγκ sehz _lohng_
declare δηλώνω THee•_loh_•noh
deduct (money) αφαιρώ
ah•feh•_roh_
defrost ξεπαγώνω
kseh•pah•_ghoh_•noh
degrees (temperature) βαθμοί
vahth•_mee_
delay n καθυστέρηση
kah•thee•_steh_•ree•see; v
καθυστερώ kah•thee•steh•_roh_

delicious νόστιμος
nohs•tee•mohs

deliver παραδίδω
pah•rah•THee•THoh

dental floss οδοντικό νήμα
oh•THohn•dee•koh nee•mah

dentist οδοντίατρος
oh•THohn•dee•ah•trohs

deodorant αποσμητικό
ah•pohz•mee•tee•koh

department store
πολυκατάστημα
poh•lee•kah•tahs•tee•mah

departure (travel) αναχώρηση
ah•nah•khoh•ree•see

departure lounge αίθουσα
αναχωρήσεων *eh•thoo•sah
ah•nah•khoh•ree•seh•ohn*

depend εξαρτώμαι
eh•ksahr•toh•meh

deposit *n (down payment)*
προκαταβολή *proh•kah•
tah•voh•lee*

describe περιγράφω
peh•reegh•rah•foh

designer σχεδιαστής
skeh•THee•ahs•tees

detergent απορρυπαντικό
ah•poh•ree•pahn•dee•koh

develop (photos) εμφανίζω
ehm•fah•nee•zoh

diabetes διαβήτης
THee•ah•vee•tees

diabetic διαβητικός
THee•ah•vee•tee•kohs

diagnosis διάγνωση
THee•ahgh•noh•see

dialing code κωδικός
koh•THee•kohs

diamond *n* διαμάντι
THiah•mahn•dee

diaper πάνα μωρού *pah•nah
moh•roo*

diarrhea διάρροια
THee•ah•ree•ah

dice *n* ζάρια *zah•riah*

dictionary λεξικό *leh•ksee•koh*

diesel ντήζελ *dee•zehl*

diet *n* δίαιτα *THee•eh•tah*

difficult δύσκολος
THee•skoh•lohs

dining room τραπεζαρία
trah•peh•zah•ree•ah

dinner βραδινό *vrah•THee•noh*

direct *v* κατευθύνω
kah•tehf•thee•noh

direction *n (instruction)* οδηγία
oh•THee•yee•ah

dirty *adj* βρώμικος
vroh•mee•kohs

disabled άτομο με ειδικές
ανάγκες *ah•toh•moh meh eh•
nahn THee•kehs ah•gehs*

discounted ticket μειωμένο
εισιτήριο *mee•oh•meh•noh
ee•see•tee•ree•oh*

dishwashing liquid λίγο υγρό
πιάτων *lee•ghoh ee•ghroh
piah•tohn*

district περιφέρεια
peh•ree•feh•ree•ah

disturb ενοχλώ *eh•noh•khloh*

diving equipment
καταδυτικός εξοπλισμός
*kah•tah•THee•tee•kohs
eh•ksoh•pleez•mohs*

divorced διαζευγμένος
THee•ah•zehv•ghmeh•nohs

dock προκυμαία
proh•kee•meh•ah

doctor γιατρός *yah•trohs*

doll κούκλα *kook•lah*

dollar δολάριο *THoh•lah•ree•oh*

door πόρτα *pohr•tah*

dosage δυσολογία
THoh•soh•loh•yee•ah

double *adj* διπλός *THeep•lohs*

double bed διπλό κρεβάτι
THeep•loh kreh•vah•tee

double room δίκλινο
δωμάτιο *THeek•lee•noh
THoh•mah•tee•oh*

downtown area κέντρο της
πόλης *kehn•droh tees poh•lees*

dozen ντουζίνα *doo•zee•nah*

dress *n* φόρεμα *foh•reh•mah*

drink *n* ποτό *poh•toh;* *v* πίνω
pee•noh

drive *v* οδηγώ *oh•THee•ghoh*

drugstore φαρμακείο
fahr•mah•kee•oh

dry cleaner καθαριστήριο
kah•thah•rees•tee•ree•oh

dubbed μεταγλωττισμένος *meh•
tahgh•loh•teez•meh•nohs*

dusty σκονισμένος
skoh•neez•meh•nohs

duty (customs) φόρος
foh•rohs; (obligation) καθήκον
kah•thee•kohn

duty-free goods αφορολόγητα
είδη *ah•foh•roh•loh•yee•tah
ee•THee*

duty-free shop κατάστημα
αφορολόγητων *kah•tahs•tee•
mah ah•foh•roh•loh•yee•tohn*

E

each κάθε ένα *kah•theh eh•nah*

ear αυτί *ahf•tee*

earache πόνος στο αυτί *poh•nohs
stoh ahf•tee*

early νωρίς *noh•rees*

east ανατολικά
ah•nah•toh•lee•kah

easy *adj* εύκολος *ehf•koh•lohs*

eat τρώω *troh•oh*

economical οικονομικός
ee•koh•noh•mee•kohs

economy class τουριστική θέση
too•ree•stee•kee theh•see

elastic ελαστικός
eh•lahs•tee•kohs

electrical outlet πρίζα *pree•zah*

e-mail ηλεκτρονικό ταχυδρομείο
*(e-mail) eh•lehk•troh•nee•koh
tah•hee•dro•mee•oh
(ee•meh•eel)*

embassy πρεσβεία prehz•_vee_•ah

emerald σμαράδι zmah•_rahgh_•THee

emergency έκτακτη ανάγκη ehk•tahk•tee ah•_nahn_•gee

emergency exit έξοδος κινδύνου eh•ksoh•THohs keen•_THEe_•noo

empty adj άδειος ah_TH_•yohs

end n τέλος _teh_•lohs; v τελειώνω teh•lee•_oh_•noh

engine μηχανή mee•khah•_nee_

England Αγγλία ahng•_lee_•ah

English adj αγγλικός ahng•lee•_kohs_; (nationality) Άγγλος ahng•_lohs_; (language) αγγλικά ahng•lee•_kah_

enjoy ευχαριστιέμαι ehf•khah•rees•_tieh_•meh

enough αρκετά ahr•keh•_tah_

entertainment guide οδηγός ψυχαγωγίας oh•_THEe_•_ghohs_ psee•khah•ghoh•_yee_•ahs

entrance fee τιμή εισόδου tee•mee ee•_soh_•THoo

epileptic επιληπτικός eh•pee•leep•tee•_kohs_

error λάθος _lah_•thohs

escalator κυλιόμενες σκάλες kee•lee•oh•meh•nehs _skah_•lehs

essential απαραίτητος ah•pah•_ree_•tee•tohs

e-ticket ηλεκτρονικό εισιτήριο ee•leh•ktroh•nee•_koh_ ee•see•_tee_•ree•oh

European Union Ευρωπαϊκή Ένωση ehv•roh•pah•ee•_kee_ eh•noh•see

euro ευρώ ehv•_roh_

evening βράδυ vrah _THee_

examination (medical) ιατρική εξέταση ee•ah•tree•_kee_ eh•_kseh_•tah•see

example παράδειγμα pah•_rah_•THeegh•mah

excess baggage υπέρβαρο ee•_pehr_•vah•roh

exchange v (money) αλλάζω ah•_lah_•zoh

exchange rate τιμή συναλλάγματος tee•_mee_ see•nah•_lahgh_•mah•tohs

excursion εκδρομή ehk•THroh•_mee_

exhibition έκθεση ehk•theh•sen

exit n έξοδος _eh_•ksoh•THohs

expensive ακριβός ahk•ree•_yohs_

expiration date ημερομηνία λήξεως ee•meh•roh•mee•_nee_•ah lee•kseh•ohs

exposure (photos) στάση _stah_•see

express (mail) εξπρές ehk•_sprehs_

extension (number) εσωτερική γραμμή eh•soh•teh•ree•_kee_ ghrah•_mee_

extra (additional) άλλο ένα ah•loh eh•nah

eye n μάτι _mah_•tee

F

fabric (cloth) ύφασμα ee•fahs•mah

face n πρόσωπο _proh_•soh•poh

facial καθαρισμός προσώπου kah•thah•ree•_mohs_ proh•_soh_•poo

facility εξυπηρέτηση eh•ksee•pee•_reh_•tee•see

faint λιποθυμώ lee•poh•thee•_moh_

fall v πέφτω _pehf_•toh

family οικογένεια ee•koh•_yeh_•nee•ah

famous διάσημος _THee_•ah•see•mohs

fan (air) ανεμιστήρας ah•neh•mees•_tee_•rahs

far adv μακριά mahk•ree•_ah_

fare εισιτήριο ee•see•_tee_•ree•oh

farm n φάρμα _fahr_•mah

fast adv γρήγορα _ghree_•ghoh•rah

fat adj (person) παχύς pah•_khees_

faucet βρύση _vree_•see

fault λάθος _lah_•thohs

favorite αγαπημένος ah•ghah•pee•_meh_•nohs

fax facility υπηρεσία φαξ ee•pee•reh•_see_•ah fahks

feed n ταΐζω tah•_ee_•zoh

female θηλυκός thee•lee•_kohs_

fence n φράχτης _frahkh_•tees

ferry φέρυ-μπωτ _feh_•ree•boht

festival φεστιβάλ fehs•tee•_vahl_

fever πυρετός pee•reh•_tohs_

fiancé αρραβωνιαστικός ah•rah•voh•niahs•tee•_kohs_

fiancée αρραβωνιαστικιά ah•rah•voh•niahs•tee•_kiah_

filling (dental) σφράγισμα _sfrah_•yeez•mah

film n (camera) φιλμ feelm

filter n φίλτρο _feel_•troh

fine adv καλά kah•_lah_; n πρόστιμο _pros_•tee•moh

finger n δάχτυλο _THakh_•tee•loh

fire n φωτιά foh•_tiah_

fire brigade [BE] πυροσβεστική pee•rohz•vehs•tee•_kee_

fire escape έξοδος κινδύνου eh•ksoh•THohs keen•_THEe_•noo

fire extinguisher πυροσβεστήρας pee•rohz•vehs•_tee_•rahs

first class πρώτη θέση _proh_•tee theh•see

first-aid kit κουτί πρώτων βοηθειών koo•_tee_ proh•tohn voh•ee•_thee_•_ohn_

fishing ψάρεμα _psah_•reh•mah

flag n σημαία see•_meh_•ah

flashlight φακός fah•_kohs_

flat adj επίπεδος eh•_pee_•peh•THohs; n διαμέρισμα THee•ah•_mehr_•ees•mah

flea ψύλλος _psee_•lohs

flight πτήση _ptee_•see

flight number αριθμός πτήσεως
ah•_reeth_•_mohs_ ptee•seh•ohs

flip-flops σαγιονάρες
sah•yoh•_nah_•rehs

flood n πλημμύρα plee•_mee_•rah

florist ανθοπωλείο
ahn•thoh•poh•_lee_•oh

flower n λουλούδι loo•_loo_•THee

flu γρίππη _ghree_•pee

flush τραβώ το καζανάκι
trah•_voh_ toh kah•zah•_nah_•kee

fly n μύγα _mee_•ghah; v πετάω
peh•_tah_•oh

follow v ακολουθώ
ah•koh•loo•_thoh_

foot πόδι poh•_THee_

football [BE] ποδόσφαιρο
poh•_THOhs_•feh•roh

footpath μονοπάτι
moh•noh•_pah_•tee

forecast n πρόβλεψη
prohv•leh•psee

foreign ξένος _kseh_•nohs

foreign currency ξένο
συνάλλαγμα _kseh_•noh
see•_nah_•lahgh•mah

forest n δάσος _THah_•sohs

forget ξεχνώ ksehkh•_noh_

form n έντυπο _ehn_•dee•poh

fortunately ευτυχώς
ehf•tee•_khohs_

forward προωθώ proh•oh•_thoh_

fountain συντριβάνι
seen•dree•_vah_•nee

free adj (available) ελεύθερος
eh•_lehf_•theh•rohs

freezer κατάψυξη
kah•_tah_•psee•ksee

frequent adj συχνός seekh•_nohs_

fresh adj φρέσκος _frehs_•kohs

friend n φίλος _fee_•lohs

frightened φοβισμένος
foh•veez•_meh_•nohs

from από ah•_poh_

front n προκυμαία
proh•kee•_meh_•ah

full adj γεμάτος yeh•_mah_•tohs

furniture έπιπλα _eh_•peep•lah

fuse n ασφάλεια ahs•_fah_•lee•ah

G

gambling τζόγος _joh_•ghohs

game (toy) παιχνίδι
pehkh•_nee_•THee

garage γκαράζ gah•_rahz_

garden n κήπος _kee_•pohs

gas βενζίνη vehn•_zee_•nee

gas station βενζινάδικο
vehn•zee•_nah_•THee•koh

gastritis γαστρίτιδα
ghahs•_tree_•tee•THah

gate (airport) έξοδος
_eh_•ksoh•THohs

genuine αυθεντικός
ahf•thehn•dee•_kohs_

get off (transport) κατεβαίνω
kah•teh•_veh_•noh

get out (of vehicle) βγαίνω
vyeh•noh

gift δώρο _THOh_•roh

gift store κατάστημα με είδη
δώρων kah•_tahs_•tee•mah meh
ee•THee _THOh_•rohn

girl κορίτσι koh•_ree_•tsee

girlfriend φίλη _fee_•lee

give δίνω _THee_•noh

glass (container) ποτήρι
poh•_tee_•ree

glasses (optical) γυαλιά
yah•_liah_

glove n γάντι _ghahn_•dee

go πηγαίνω pee•_yeh_•noh

gold n χρυσός khree•_sohs_

golf γκόλφ gohlf

golf course γήπεδο γκολφ
yee•peh•THoh gohlf

good καλός kah•_lohs_

grass γρασίδι ghrah•_see_•THee

gratuity φιλοδώρημα
fee•loh•_THOh_•ree•mah

greasy (hair, skin) λιπαρός
lee•pah•_rohs_

Greece Ελλάδα eh•_lah_•THah

Greek adj ελληνικός
eh•lee•nee•_kohs_; (nationality) Έλληνας eh•_lee_•nahs

greengrocer [BE] οπωροπωλείο
oh•poh•roh•poh•_lee_•oh

ground (earth) έδαφος
eh•_THah_•fohs

group n γκρουπ groop

guarantee n εγγύηση
eh•_gee_•ee•see; v εγγυώμαι
eh•gee•_oh_•meh

guide book τουριστικό
οδηγός too•ree•stee•_koh_
oh•THee•_ghohs_

guided tour ξενάγηση
kseh•_nah_•yee•see

guitar κιθάρα kee•_thah_•rah

gynecologist γυναικολόγος
yee•neh•koh•_loh_•ghohs

H

hair μαλλιά mah•_liah_

hairbrush βούρτσα _voor_•tsah

hair dresser κομμωτήριο
koh•moh•_tee_•ree•oh

hair dryer σεσουάρ
seh•soo•_ahr_

half μισός mee•_sohs_

hammer σφυρί sfee•_ree_

hand n χέρι _kheh_•ree

hand luggage αποσκευές χειρός
ah•pohs•keh•_vehs_ khee•_rohs_

handbag τσάντα _tsahn_•dah

handicraft λαϊκή τέχνη
lah•ee•_kee_ tehkh•nee

handicapped-accessible toilet
προσβάσιμη τουαλέτα για
ανάπηρους prohs•_vah_•see•mee
too•ah•_leh_•tah yah
ah•_nah_•pee•roos

handkerchief χαρτομάντηλο
khah•rtoh•_mahn_•dee•loh

handle n πόμολο poh•_moh_•loh

hanger κρεμάστρα
kreh•_mahs_•trah

harbor n λιμάνι *lee•mah•nee*
hat καπέλο *kah•peh•loh*
have (possession) έχω *eh•khoh*
have to (obligation) οφείλω
oh•fee•loh
head n κεφάλι *keh•fah•lee*
headache πονοκέφαλος
poh•noh•keh•fah•lohs
health food store κατάστημα
με υγιεινές τροφές
*kah•tahs•tee•mah meh
ee•yee•ehs•nehs troh•fehs*
health insurance ασφάλεια
υγείας *ahs•fah•lee•ah
ee•yee•ahs*
hearing aid ακουστικό
βαρηκοΐας *ah•koo•stee•koh
vah•ree•koh•ee•ahs*
heart v καρδιά *kahr•THee•ah*
heart attack καρδιακό
έμφραγμα *kahr•THee•ah•koh
ehm•frahgh•mah*
heat wave καύσωνας
kahf•soh•nahs
heater (water) θερμοσίφωνας
thehr•moh•see•foh•nahs
heating θέρμανση
thehr•mahn•see
heavy βαρύς *vah•rees*
height ύψος *ee•psohs*
helicopter ελικόπτερο
eh•lee•kohp•teh•roh
help n βοήθεια *voh•ee•thee•ah;*
v βοηθώ *voh•ee•thoh*
here εδώ *eh•THoh*
highway εθνική οδός
ehth•nee•kee oh•THohs
hike v κάνω πεζοπορία *kah•noh
peh•zoh•poh•ree•ah*
hill λόφος *loh•fohs*
hire [BE] v νοικιάζω *nee•kiah•zoh*
history ιστορία *ee•stoh•ree•ah*
hitchhiking οτοστόπ
oh•toh•stohp
hobby (pastime) χόμπυ
khoh•bee

hold on περιμένω
peh•ree•meh•noh
hole (in clothes) τρύπα *tree•pah*
holiday [BE] διακοπές
THee•ah•koh•pehs
honeymoon μήνας του μέλιτος
mee•nahs too meh•lee•tohs
horse track ιπποδρόμιο
ee•poh•THroh•mee•oh
hospital νοσοκομείο
noh•soh•koh•mee•oh
hot (weather) ζεστός *zehs•tohs*
hot spring θερμή πηγή
thehr•mee pee•yee
hotel ξενοδοχείο
kseh•noh•THoh•khee•oh
household articles είδη
οικιακής χρήσεως *ee•THee
ee•kee•ah•kees khree•seh•ohs*
husband σύζυγος *see•zee•ghohs*

I

ice n πάγος *pah•ghohs*
identification ταυτότητα
tahf•toh•tee•tah
illegal παράνομος
pah•rah•noh•mohs
illness αρρώστεια
ahr•ohs•tee•ah
imitation απομίμηση
ah•poh•mee•mee•see
immediately αμέσως
ah•meh•sohs
impressive εντυπωσιακός
ehn•dee•poh•see•ah•kohs
included συμπεριλαμβάνεται
*seem•beh•ree•lahm•vah•
neh•teh*
indigestion δυσπεψία
THehs•peh•psee•ah
indoor εσωτερικός
eh•soh•teh•ree•kohs
indoor pool εσωτερική
πισίνα *eh•soh•teh•ree•kee
pee•see•nah*
inexpensive φτηνός *ftee•nohs*

infected μολυσμένος
moh•leez•meh•nohs
inflammation φλεγμονή
flegh•moh•nee
information πληροφορίες
plee•roh•foh•ree•ehs
information office γραφείο
πληροφοριών *ghrah•fee•oh
plee•roh•foh•ree•ohn*
injection ένεση *eh•neh•see*
injured τραυματισμένος
trahv•mah•teez•meh•nohs
innocent αθώος *ah•thoh•ohs*
insect bite τσίμπημα από έντομο
*tseem•bee•mah ah•poh
ehn•doh•moh*
insect repellent
εντομοαπωθητικό *ehn•doh•
moh•ah•poh•thee•tee•koh*
inside μέσα *meh•sah*
insist επιμένω *eh•pee•meh•noh*
insomnia αϋπνία
ah•eep•nee•ah
instruction οδηγία
oh•THee•yee•ah
insulin ινσουλίνη
een•soo•lee•nee
insurance ασφάλεια
ahs•fah•lee•ah
insurance certificate
πιστοποιητικό ασφάλειας
*pees•toh•pee•ee•tee•koh
ahs•fah•lee•ahs*
insurance claim ασφάλεια
αποζημίωσης *ahs•fah•lee•ah
ah•poh•zee•mee•oh•sees*
**insurance com-
pany** ασφαλιστική εταιρία
*ahs•fah•lees•tee•kee
eh•teh•ree•ah*
interest rate επιτόκιο
eh•pee•toh•kee•oh
interesting ενδιαφέρων
ehn•THee•ah•feh•rohn
international διεθνής
THee•eth•nees

**International Student
 Card** διεθνής φοιτητική
 κάρτα *Thee•ehth•nees
 fee•tee•tee•kee kahr•tah*
internet ίντερνετ *ee•nteh•rnet*
internet cafe ίντερνετ καφέ
 ee•nteh•rnet kah•feh
interpreter διερμηνέας
 THee•ehrm•ee•neh•ahs
interval διάλειμμα
 THee•ah•lee•mah
introduce συστήνω *see•stee•noh*
introductions συστάσεις
 see•stah•sees
invitation πρόσκληση
 prohs•klee•see
invite v προσκαλώ *prohs•kah•loh*
iodine ιώδειο *ee•oh•THee•oh*
iron n σίδερο *see•THeh•roh*; v
 σιδερώνω *see•THeh•roh•noh*
itemized bill αναλυτικός
 λογαριασμός *ah•nah•lee•tee•
 kohs loh•ghahr•yahz•mohs*

J

jacket σακάκι *sah•kah•kee*
jammed σφηναγμένος
 sfee•nah•meh•nohs
jar n βάζο *vah•zoh*
jaw σαγόνι *sah•ghoh•nee*
jeans μπλου-τζην *bloo•jeen*
jellyfish μέδουσα *meh•THoo•sah*
jet-ski τζετ-σκι *jeht•skee*
jeweler κοσμηματοπωλείο *kohz•
 mee•mah•toh•poh•lee•oh*
job δουλειά *THoo•liah*
jogging τζόγκινγκ *joh•geeng*
joke n ανέκδοτο
 ah•nehk•THoh•toh
journey ταξίδι *tah•ksee•THee*
junction (intersection) κόμβος
 kohm•vohs

K

keep v κρατώ *krah•toh*
key n κλειδί *klee•THee*

key card κάρτα-κλειδί
 kahr•tah•klee•dee
key ring μπρελόκ *breh•lohk*
kidney νεφρό *nehf•roh*
kind είδος *ee•THohs*
king βασιλιάς *vah•see•liahs*
kiosk περίπτερο
 peh•ree•pteh•roh
kiss n φιλί *fee•lee*; v φιλώ
 fee•loh
kitchen χαρτί κουζίνας *khah•rtee
 koo•zee•nahs*
knapsack σάκκος *sah•kohs*
knee γόνατο *ghoh•nah•toh*
knife μαχαίρι *mah•kheh•ree*
know γνωρίζω *ghnoh•ree•zoh*

L

label n ετικέτα *eh•tee•keh•tah*
ladder σκάλα *skah•lah*
lake λίμνη *leem•nee*
lamp λάμπα *lahm•bah*
land n γη *ghee*; v προσγειώνομαι
 prohz•yee•oh•noh•meh
language course μάθημα ξένης
 γλώσσας *mah•thee•mah
 kseh•nees ghloh•sahs*
large adj μεγάλος *meh•ghah•lohs*
last τελευταίος *teh•lehf•teh•ohs*
late adv αργά *ahr•ghah*
laugh v γελώ *yeh•loh*
laundry facility πλυντήριο
 pleen•dee•rec•oh
lavatory μπάνιο *bah•nioh*
lawyer δικηγόρος
 THee•kee•ghoh•rohs
laxative καθαρτικό
 kah•thahr•tee•koh
learn μαθαίνω *mah•theh•noh*
leave v (depart) φεύγω *fehv•ghoh*;
 (let go) αφήνω *ah•fee•noh*
left adj αριστερός
 ah•rees•teh•rohs; adv
 αριστερά *ah•rees•teh•rah*
leg πόδι *poh•THee*
legal νόμιμος *noh•mee•mohs*

lend δανείζω *THah•nee•zoh*
length μήκος *mee•kohs*
lens φακός *fah•kohs*
lens cap κάλυμμα φακού
 kah•lee•mah fah•koo
less λιγότερο *lee•ghoh•teh•roh*
letter γράμμα *grah•mah*
level (even) επίπεδο
 eh•pee•peh•THoh
library βιβλιοθήκη
 veev•lee•oh•thee•kee
lie down ξαπλώνω *ksah•ploh•noh*
life boat ναυαγοσωστική λέμβος
 *nah•vah•ghoh•sos•tee•kee
 lehm•vohs*
lifeguard ναυαγοσώστης
 nah•vah•ghoh•sohs•tees
life jacket σωσίβιο
 soh•see•vee•oh
lift [BE] n (elevator) ασανσέρ
 ah•sahn•sehr
lift pass άδεια σκι *ah•THee•ah
 skee*
light adj (color) ανοιχτός
 ah•neekh•tohs; n (electric)
 φως *fohs*
light bulb λάμπα *lahm•bah*
lighter adj ανοιχτότερος
 ah•neekh•toh•teh•rohs; n
 αναπτήρας *ah•nahp•tee•rahs*
lighthouse φάρος *fah•rohs*
lights (car) φώτα *foh•tah*
line n (subway) γραμμή
 ghrah•mee
lips χείλη *khee•lee*
lipstick κραγιόν *krah•yohn*
liter λίτρο *lee•troh*
little μικρός *meek•rohs*
liver συκώτι *see•koh•tee*
living room σαλόνι *sah•loh•nee*
local τοπικός *toh•pee•kohs*
location (space) θέση *theh•see*
lock n (door) κλειδαριά
 klee•THahr•yah; (river,
 canal) φράγμα *frahgh•mah*; v
 κλειδώνω *klee•THoh•noh*

long *adj* μακρύς *mak•rees*

long-distance bus
υπεραστικό λεωφορείο
ee•peh•rahs•tee•koh
leh•oh•foh•ree•oh

long-distance call
υπεραστικό τηλεφώνημα
ee•pehr•ahs•tee•koh
tee•leh•foh•nee•mah

long-sighted [BE] πρεσβύωπας
prehz•vee•oh•pahs

look *v* κοιτάω *kee•tah•oh*

look for ψάχνω *psahkh•noh*

loose (fitting) φαρδύς
fahr•Thees

loss *n* απώλεια *ah•poh•lee•ah*

lotion λοσιόν *loh•siohn*

loud *adj* δυνατός *THee•nah•tohs*

love *v* αγαπώ *ah•ghah•poh*

lower *adj (berth)* κάτω *kah•toh*

lubricant λιπαντικό
lee•pahn•dee•koh

luck τύχη *tee•khee*

luggage αποσκευές
ah•pohs•keh•vehs

luggage cart καροτσάκι
αποσκευών *kah•roh•tsah•kee*
ah•pohs•keh•vohn

luggage locker θυρίδα
thee•ree•THah

lukewarm χλιαρός *khlee•ah•rohs*

lump *n* οβώλος *svoh•lohs;*
(medical) εξόγκωμα
eh•ksoh•goh•mah

lunch *n* μεσημεριανό
meh•see•mehr•yah•noh

lung πνεύμονας *pnehv•moh•nahs*

luxury πολυτέλεια
poh•lee•teh•lee•ah

M

magazine περιοδικό
peh•ree•oh•THee•koh

magnificent μεγαλοπρεπής
meh•ghah•lohp•reh•pees

mailbox ταχυδρομικό κουτί *tah•*
kheeTH•roh•mee•koh koo•tee

mail *n* αλληλογραφία
ah•lee•lohgh•rah•fee•ah

main κύριος *kee•ree•ohs*

make-up μακιγιάζ *mah•kee•yahz*

man (male) άνδρας *ahn•THrahs*

manager διευθυντής
THee•ehf•theen•dees

manicure μανικιούρ
mah•nee•kioor

manual (car) χειροκίνητος
khee•roh•kee•nee•tohs

map *n* χάρτης *khahr•tees*

market *n* αγορά *ah•ghoh•rah*

married παντρεμένος
pahn•dreh•meh•nohs

mask *n (diving)* μάσκα *mahs•kah*

mass *n (church)* λειτουργία
lee•toor•yee•ah

massage *n* μασάζ *mah•sahz*

match *n (sport)* αγώνας
ah•ghoh•nahs; (fire starter)
σπίρτο *speer•toh*

maybe ίσως *ee•sohs*

meal γεύμα *yehv•mah*

mean *v* σημαίνω *see•meh•noh*

measure *v* μετρώ *meht•roh*

measurement μέτρηση
meh•tree•see

medication φάρμακα
fahr•mah•kah

meet συναντώ *see•nahn•doh*

memorial μνημείο *mnee•mee•oh*

mend διορθώνω
THee•ohr•thoh•noh

menstrual cramp πόνος
περιόδου *puh•nohs*
peh•ree•oh•THoo

mention αναφέρω
ah•nah•feh•roh

message *n* μήνυμα
mee•nee•mah

metal *n* μέταλλο *meh•tah•loh*

microwave (oven) φούρνος
μικροκυμάτων *foor•nohs*
mee•kroh•kee•mah•tohn

migraine ημικρανία
ee•mee•krah•nee•ah

mileage χιλιόμετρα
khee•lioh•meh•trah

mini-bar μίνι-μπαρ
mee•nee•bahr

minimart παντοπωλείο
pahn•doh•poh•lee•oh

minimum ελάχιστος
eh•lah•khees•tohs

minute *n (time)* λεπτό *lehp•toh*

mirror *n* καθρέφτης
kah•threhf•tees

mistake λάθος *lah•thohs*

misunderstanding παρεξήγηση
pah•eh•ksee•yee•see

mobile phone [BE] κινητό
kee•nee•toh

modern μοντέρνος
moh•deh•rnohs

moisturizer *(cream)* ενυδατική
κρέμα *eh•nee•THah•tee•kee*
kreh•mah

money χρήματα *khree•mah•tah*

money order
ταχυδρομική επιταγή
tah•kheeTH•roh•mee•kee
eh•pee•tah•yee

money-belt ζώνη για χρήματα
zoh•nee yah khree•mah•tah

monument μνημείο
mnee•mee•oh

moped μοτοποδήλατο
moh•toh•poh•THee•lah•toh

more παραπάνω
pah•rah•pah•noh

morning πρωί *proh•ee*

mosquito κουνούπι *koo•noo•pee*

mosquito bite τσίμπημα
κουνουπιού *tseem•bee•mah*
koo•noo•piooh

motorboat εξωλέμβιο
eh•ksoh•lehm•vee•oh

motorway [BE] εθνική οδός
ehth•nee•kee oh•THohs

mountain βουνό *voo•noh*

moustache μουστάκι
moos•<u>tah</u>•kee

mouth n στόμα <u>stoh</u>•mah

move v (room) μετακομίζω
meh•tah•koh•<u>mee</u>•zoh

movie ταινία teh•<u>nee</u>•ah

movie theater κινηματογράφος
kee•nee•mah•tohgh•<u>rah</u>•fohs

much πολύ poh•<u>lee</u>

muscle n μυς mees

museum μουσείο moo•<u>see</u>•oh

music μουσική moo•see•<u>kee</u>

musician μουσικός
moo•see•<u>kohs</u>

must v πρέπει <u>preh</u>•pee

N

nail salon σαλόνι νυχιών
sah•<u>loh</u>•nee nee•<u>khiohn</u>

name n όνομα <u>oh</u>•noh•mah

napkin πετσέτα peh•<u>tseh</u>•tah

nappy [BE] πάνα μωρού <u>pah</u>•nah
moh•<u>roo</u>

narrow στενός steh•<u>nohs</u>

national εθνικός eth•nee•<u>kohs</u>

nationality υπηκοότητα
ee•pee•koh•<u>oh</u>•tee•tah

nature φύση <u>fee</u>•see

nature reserve εθνικός δρυμός
eth•nee•<u>kohs</u> THree•<u>mohs</u>

nature trail μονοπάτι
moh•noh•<u>pah</u>•tee

nausea ναυτία nahf•<u>tee</u>•ah

near adv κοντά kohn•<u>dah</u>

nearby εδώ κοντά eh•<u>THoh</u>
kohn•<u>dah</u>

necessary απαραίτητος
ah•pah•<u>reh</u>•tee•luhs

necklace κολλιέ koh•<u>lieh</u>

need v χρειάζομαι
khree•<u>ah</u>•zoh•meh

neighbor n γείτονας
<u>yee</u>•toh•nahs

nerve νεύρο <u>nehv</u>•roh

never ποτέ poh•<u>teh</u>

new καινούργιος keh•<u>noor</u>•yohs

newspaper εφημερίδα
eh•fee•meh•<u>ree</u>•THah

newsstand περίπτερο
peh•<u>ree</u>•pteh•roh

next επόμενος eh•<u>poh</u>•meh•nohs

next to δίπλα <u>THeep</u>•lah

night νύχτα <u>neekh</u>•tah

night club νυχτερινό κέντρο
neekh•teh•ree•<u>noh</u> <u>kehn</u>•droh

noisy θορυβώδης
thoh•ree•<u>voh</u>•THees

none adj κανένας kah•<u>neh</u>•nahs

non-smoking μη καπνίζοντες
mee kap•<u>nee</u>•zohn•dehs

north βόρεια <u>voh</u>•ree•ah

nose n μύτη <u>mee</u>•tee

nudist beach παραλία
γυμνιστών pah•rah•<u>lee</u>•ah
yeem•nees•<u>tohn</u>

nurse n νοσοκόμα
noh•soh•<u>koh</u>•mah

O

occupied κατειλημένος
kah•tee•lee•<u>meh</u>•nohs

office γραφείο ghrah•<u>fee</u>•oh

old adj (thing) παλιός pah•<u>liohs</u>;
(person) γέρικος <u>yeh</u>•ree•kohs

old town παλιά πόλη pah•<u>liah</u>
<u>poh</u>•lee

old-fashioned ντεμοντέ
deh•mohn•<u>deh</u>

once μια φορά miah foh•<u>rah</u>

one-way ticket απλό εισιτήριο
ahp•<u>loh</u> ee•see•<u>tee</u>•ree•oh

open adj ανοιχτός ah•neekh•<u>tohs</u>;
v ανοίγω ah•<u>nee</u>•ghoh

opening hours ώρες λειτουργίας
<u>oh</u>•rehs lee•toor•<u>yee</u>•ahs

opera όπερα <u>oh</u>•peh•rah

opposite απέναντι
ah•<u>peh</u>•nahn•dee

optician οφθαλμίατρος
ohf•thahl•mee•<u>aht</u>•rohs

orchestra ορχήστρα
ohr•<u>khees</u>•trah

order v παραγγέλνω
pah•rah•<u>gehl</u>•noh

organized οργανωμένος
ohr•ghah•noh•<u>meh</u>•nohs

others άλλα <u>ah</u>•lah

out adv έξω <u>eh</u>•ksoh

outdoor εξωτερικός
eh•ksoh•teh•ree•<u>kohs</u>

outside adj έξω eh•<u>ksoh</u>

oval οβάλ oh•<u>vahl</u>

oven φούρνος <u>foor</u>•nohs

over there εκεί eh•<u>kee</u>

overnight (package) ένα βράδυ
eh•nah vrah•THee

owe χρωστώ khroh•<u>stoh</u>

owner κάτοχος <u>kah</u>•toh•khohs

P

pacifier πιπίλα pee•<u>pee</u>•lah

pack v (baggage) φτιάχνω τις
βαλίτσες ftee•<u>ahkh</u>•noh tees
vah•<u>lee</u>•tsehs

paddling pool [BE] ρηχή πισίνα
ree•<u>khee</u> pee•see•<u>nah</u>

padlock λουκέτο loo•<u>keh</u>•toh

pain n πόνος <u>poh</u>•nohs

painkiller παυσίπονο
pahf•<u>see</u>•poh•noh

paint v ζωγραφίζω
zohgh•rah•<u>fee</u>•zoh

pair ζευγάρι zehv•<u>ghah</u>•ree

pajamas πυτζάμες pee•<u>jah</u>•mehs

palace ανάκτορα
ah•<u>nahk</u>•toh•rah

panorama πανόραμα
pah•<u>noh</u>•rah•mah

pants παντελόνι
pahn•deh•<u>loh</u>•nee

paper χαρτί khar•<u>tee</u>

paralysis παραλυσία
pah•rah•lee•<u>see</u>•ah

parcel πακέτο pah•<u>keh</u>•toh

parents γονείς ghoh•<u>nees</u>

park n πάρκο <u>pahr</u>•koh

parking lot χώρος στάθμευσης
<u>khoh</u>•rohs <u>stahth</u>•mehf•sees

parking meter παρκόμετρο
pahr•koh•meht•roh

party n (social gathering) πάρτυ
pah•rtee

pass v περνώ pehr•noh

passenger επιβάτης
eh•pee•vah•tees

passport διαβατήριο
THiah•vah•tee•ree•oh

pastry store ζαχαροπλαστείο
zah•khah•rohp•lahs•tee•oh

path μονοπάτι moh•noh•pah•tee

pay v πληρώνω plee•roh•noh

payment πληρωμή plee•roh•mee

peak n κορυφή koh•ree•fee

pearl μαργαριτάρι
mahr•ghah•ree•tah•ree

pebbly (beach) με χαλίκια meh
khah•lee•kiah

pedestrian crossing διάβαση
πεζών THee•ah•vah•see
peh•zohn

pedestrian zone πεζόδρομος
peh•zohnTH•roh•mohs

pen n στυλό stee•loh

per την teen

perhaps ίσως ee•sohs

period (menstrual) περίοδος
peh•ree•oh•THohs; (time)
χρονική περίοδος khroh•
nee•kee peh•ree•oh•Thohs

permit n άδεια ah•THee•ah

petrol [BE] βενζίνη
vehn•zee•nee

pewter κασίτερος
kah•see•teh•rohs

phone n τηλέφωνο
tee•leh•foh•noh

phone call τηλεφώνημα
tee•leh•foh•nee•mah

phone card τηλεκάρτα
tee•leh•kahr•tah

photo v φωτογραφία
foh•tohgh•rah•fee•ah

photocopier φωτοτυπικό
foh•toh•tee•pee•koh

phrase n φράση frah•see

pick up παίρνω pehr•noh

picnic area περιοχή για
πικνίκ peh•ree•oh•khee yah
peek•neek

piece τεμάχιο teh•mah•khee•oh

pillow μαξιλάρι
mah•ksee•lah•ree

pillow case μαξιλαροθήκη
mah•ksee•lah•roh•thee•kee

pipe (smoking) πίπα pee•pah

piste [BE] μονοπάτι

pizzeria πιτσαρία
pee•tsah•ree•ah

plan n σχέδιο skheh•THee•oh

plane n αεροπλάνο
ah•eh•rohp•lah•noh

plant n φυτό fee•toh

plastic wrap διαφανή
μεμβράνη THee•ah•fah•nee
mehm•vrah•nee

platform αποβάθρα
ah•poh•vahth•rah

platinum πλατίνα plah•tee•nah

play v (games) παίζω pehz•zoh;
(music) παίζω pehz•zoh

playground παιδική χαρά
peh•THee•kee khah•rah

pleasant ευχάριστος
ehf•khah•rees•tohs

plug n πρίζα pree•zah

point n σημείο see•mee•oh; v
δείχνω THeekh•noh

poison n δηλητήριο
THee•lee•tee•ree•oh

poisonous δηλητηριώδης
THee•lee•tee•ree•oh•THees

police n αστυνομία
ah•stee•noh•mee•ah

police station αστυνομικό
τμήμα ah•stee•noh•mee•koh
tmee•mah

pond n λιμνούλα leem•noo•lah

popular δημοφιλής
THee•moh•fee•lees

porter αχθοφόρος
ahkh•thoh•foh•rohs

portion n μερίδα meh•ree•THah

possible πιθανός pee•thah•nohs

postbox [BE] ταχυδρομικό κουτί
tah•kheeTH•roh•mee•koh
koo•tee

post card καρτποστάλ
kahrt•poh•stahl

post office ταχυδρομείο
tah•kheeTH•roh•mee•oh

pottery αγγειοπλαστική
ahn•gee•oh•plahs•tee•kee

pound (sterling) λίρα lee•rah

pregnant έγκυος eh•gee•ohs

prescribe συνταγογραφώ
seen•dah•ghoh•ghrah•foh

prescription συνταγή γιατρού
seen•dah•yee yaht•roo

present δώρο THoh•roh

press v σιδερώνω
see•THeh•roh•noh

pretty πι' όμορφος
oh•mohr•fohs

prison n φυλακή fee•lah•kee

private bathroom ιδιωτικό
μπάνιο ee•THee•oh•tee•koh
bah•nioh

problem πρόβλημα
prohv•lee•mah

program n πρόγραμμα
prohgh•rah•mah

program of events πρόγραμμα
θεαμάτων prohgh•rah•mah
theh•ah•mah•tohn

prohibited απαγορευμένος
ah•pah•ghoh•rehv•meh•nohs

pronounce προφέρω
proh•feh•roh

public δημόσιος
THee•moh•see•ohs

public holiday αργία
ahr•yee•ah

pump n τρόμπα troh•mbah

purpose σκοπός skoh•pohs

put v βάζω vah•zoh

Q

quality ποιότητα *pee•oh•tee•tah*

quantity ποσότητα
poh•soh•tee•tah

quarantine n καραντίνα
kah•rahn•dee•nah

quarter (quantity) ένα τέταρτο
eh•nah teh•tah•rtoh

quay αποβάθρα *ah•poh•vath•rah*

question n ερώτηση
eh•roh•tee•see

queue [BE] v περιμένω στην ουρά *peh•ree•meh•noh steen oo•rah*

quick γρήγορος *ghree•ghoh•rohs*

quiet adj ήσυχος *ee•see•khohs*

R

racket (tennis, squash) ρακέτα
rah•keh•tah

radio n ραδιόφωνο
rah•THee•oh•foh•noh

railway station [BE]
σιδηροδρομικός σταθμός
see•THee•rohTH•roh•mee•kohs stahth•mohs

rain n βροχή *vroh•khee*; v βρέχει
vreh•khee

raincoat αδιάβροχο
ah•THee•ahv•roh•khoh

rapids ρεύμα ποταμού *rehv•mah poh•tah•moo*

rare (unusual) σπάνιος
spah•nee•ohs

rash n εξάνθημα
eh•ksahn•thee•mah

ravine ρεματιά *reh•mah•tiah*

razor ξυραφάκι *ksee•rah•fah•kee*

razor blade ξυραφάκι
ksee•rah•fah•kee

ready adj έτοιμος *eh•tee•mohs*

real (genuine) γνήσιος
ghee•see•ohs; **(true)** αληθινός
ah•lee•thee•nohs

receipt απόδειξη
ah•poh•THee•ksee

reception (hotel) ρεσεψιόν
reh•seh•psiohn

recommend συστήνω
sees•tee•noh

reduction έκπτωση
ehk•ptoh•see

refund n επιστροφή
χρημάτων *eh•pees•troh•fee khree•mah•tohn*

region περιοχή *peh•ree•oh•khee*

registration number αριθμός
κυκλοφορίας *ah•reeth•mohs kee•kloh•foh•ree•ahs*

religion θρησκεία *three•skee•ah*

remember θυμάμαι
thee•mah•meh

rent v νοικιάζω *nee•kiah•zoh*

repair n επισκευή *eh•pee•skeh•vee*; v επισκευάζω
eh•pee•skeh•vah•zoh

repeat v επαναλαμβάνω
eh•pah•nah•lahm•vah•noh

replacement part ανταλλακτικό
ahn•dah•lahk•tee•koh

report v αναφέρω
ah•nah•feh•roh

restaurant εστιατόριο
ehs•tee•ah•toh•ree•oh

restroom τουαλέτα
too•ah•leh•tah

retired συνταξιούχος
seen•dah•ksee•oo•khohs

return ticket [BE] εισιτήριο με
επιστροφή *ee•see•tee•ree•oh meh eh•pee•stroh•fee*

reverse the charges με
χρέωση του καλούμενου
meh khreh•oh•see too kah•loo•meh•noo

revolting αηδιαστικός
ah•ee•THee•ah•stee•kohs

rib πλευρό *plehv•roh*

right adj **(correct)** σωστός
soh•stohs; **(side)** δεξιός
THeh•ksee•ohs

river ποταμός *poh•tah•mohs*

road δρόμος *THroh•mohs*

road assistance οδική βοήθεια
oh•THee•kee voh•ee•thee•ah

road sign πινακίδα
pee•nah•kee•Thah

robbery ληστεία *lees•tee•ah*

rock n βράχος *vrah•khohs*

rock climbing αναρρίχηση
ah•nah•ree•khee•see

romantic ρομαντικός
roh•mahn•dee•kohs

roof n στέγη *steh•yee*

room n δωμάτιο *THoh•mah•tee•oh*

room service υπηρεσία
δωματίου *ee•pee•reh•see•ah THoh•mah•tee•oh*

rope n σχοινί *skhee•nee*

round adj στρογγυλός
strohn•gkee•lohs; n *(of golf)*
παιχνίδι *pehkh•nee•THee*

round-trip ticket εισιτήριο με
επιστροφή *ee•see•tee•ree•oh meh eh•pee•stroh•fee*

route n διαδρομή
THee•ahTH•roh•mee

rowing κωπηλασία
koh•pee•lah•see•ah

rubbish [BE] σκουπίδια
skoo•pee•THyah

rude αγενής *ah•yeh•nees*

rug χαλί *khah•lee*

run v τρέχω *treh•khoh*

rush hour ώρα αιχμής *oh•rah ehkh•mees*

S

safe adj **(not dangerous)** ασφαλής
ahs•fah•lees

sailing boat ιστιοπλοϊκό
ees•tee•oh•ploh•ee•koh

sales tax ΦΠΑ *fee•pee•ah*

same ίδιος *ee•THee•ohs*

sand άμμος *ah•mohs*

sandals πέδιλα *peh•THee•lah*

sandy (beach) με άμμο *meh ah•moh*

sanitary napkin σερβιέτα
sehr•vee•eh•tah

satin σατέν *sah•tehn*

saucepan κατσαρόλα
kah•tsah•roh•lah

sauna σάουνα *sah•oo•nah*

scarf κασκόλ *kahs•kohl*

scissors ψαλίδι *psah•lee•THee*

scratch γρατζουνιά
ghrah•joo•niah

screw n βίδα *vee•THah*

screwdriver κατσαβίδι
kah•tsah•vee•THee

sea θάλασσα *thah•lah•sah*

seafront προκυμαία
proh•kee•meh•ah

seat n θέση *theh•see*

second-hand shop κατάστημα
μεταχειρισμένων ειδών *kah•
tah•stee•mah meh•tah•
khee•reez•meh•nohn ee•THohn*

sedative ηρεμιστικό
ee•reh•mee•stee•koh

see βλέπω *vleh•poh*

send στέλνω *stehl•noh*

senior citizen ηλικιωμένος
ee•lee•kee•oh•see

separately ξεχωριστά
kseh•khoh•ree•stah

service n (business) υπηρεσία
ee•pee•reh•see•ah; (mass)
λειτουργία *lee•toor•yee•ah*

service charge χρέωση
υπηρεσίας *khreh•oh•see
ee•pee•reh•see•ahs*

sewer υπόνομος
ee•poh•noh•mohs

shade (color) απόχρωση
ah•pohkh•roh•see; (darkness) σκιά *skee•ah*

shampoo n σαμπουάν
sahm•poo•ahn

shape n σχήμα *skhee•mah*

shaving cream κρέμα
ξυρίσματος *kreh•mah
ksee•reez•mah•tohs*

shelf n ράφι *rah•fee*

ship n πλοίο *plee•oh*

shirt πουκάμισο
poo•kah•mee•soh

shock (electric)
ηλεκτροπληξία
ee•leh•ktroh•plee•ksee•ah

shoe παπούτσι *pah•poo•tsee*

shoe polish βερνίκι
παπουτσιών *vehr•nee•kee
pah•poo•tsiohn*

shoe repair επισκευή
παπουτσιών *eh•pee•skeh•vee
pah•poo•tsiohn*

shoe store κατάστημα
υποδημάτων
*kah•stee•mah
ee•poh•THee•mah•tohn*

shop (store) κατάστημα
kah•stee•mah

shopping mall εμπορικό κέντρο
ehm•boh•ree•koh keh•ntroh

shore n ακτή *ahk•tee*

short adj κοντός *kohn•dohs*

shorts n σορτς *sohrts*

short-sighted [BE] μύωπας
mee•oh•pahs

shoulder n (anatomy) ώμος
oh•mohs

show δείχνω *THeekh•noh*

shower n ντους *dooz*

shower gel αφρόλουτρο για
ντους *ahf•roh•loot•roh
yah dooz*

shut adj κλειστός *klees•tohs*

sick adj άρρωστος *ah•rohs•tohs*

side (of road) μεριά *mehr•yah*

sightseeing sight αξιοθέατο
ah•ksee•oh•theh•ah•toh

sightseeing tour ξενάγηση στα
αξιοθέατα *kseh•nah•yee•see
stah ah•ksee•oh•theh•ah•tah*

sign (road) σήμα *see•mah*

silk μετάξι *meh•tah•ksee*

silver ασήμι *ah•see•mee*

simple απλός *ahp•lohs*

single (not married) ελεύθερος
eh•lehf•theh•rohs

single room μονόκλινο
δωμάτιο *moh•noh•klee•noh
THoh•mah•tee•oh*

single ticket [BE] απλό
εισιτήριο *ahp•loh
ee•see•tee•ree•oh*

sink (bathroom) νιπτήρας
nee•ptee•rahs

sit κάθομαι *kah•thoh•meh*

size n μέγεθος *meh•yeh•thohs*

skates παγοπέδιλα
pah•ghoh•peh•THee•lah

skating rink παγοδρόμιο
pah•ghohiTH•roh•mee•oh

ski boots μπότες του σκι
boh•tehs too skee

ski poles μπαστούνια του σκι
bahs•too•niah too skee

ski school σχολή σκι *skhoh•lee
skee*

skiing σκι *skee*

skin n δέρμα *Thehr•mah*

skirt φούστα *foo•stah*

sleep v κοιμάμαι *kee•mah•meh*

sleeping bag υπνόσακκος
ee•pnoh•sah•kohs

sleeping car βαγκόν-λι
vah•gohn•lee

sleeping pill υπνωτικό χάπι
eep•noh•tee•koh khah•pee

slippers παντόφλες
pahn•dohf•lehs

slope (ski) πλαγιά *plah•yah*

slow adj αργός *ahr•ghohs*

small μικρός *meek•rohs*

smell v μυρίζω *mee•ree•zoh*

smoke v καπνίζω *kahp•nee•zoh*

smoking area περιοχή για
καπνίζοντες *peh•ee•oh•khee
yah kahp•nee•zohn•dehs*

snack bar κυλικείο
kee•lee•kee•oh

sneakers αθλητικά παπούτσια
ath•lee•tee•kah pah•poo•tsia

snorkeling equipment
εξοπλισμό για ελεύθερη
κατάδυση eh•ksohp•leez•moh
yah eh•lehf•theh•ree
kah•tah•THee•see

snow ν χιονίζει khioh•nee•zee

soap n σαπούνι sah•poo•nee

soccer ποδόσφαιρο
poh•THOhs•feh•roh

socket πρίζα pree•zah

socks κάλτσες kah•tsehs

sofa καναπές kah•nah•pehs

sole (shoes) σόλα soh•lah

something κάτι kah•tee

sometimes μερικές φορές
meh•ree•kehs foh•rehs

soon σύντομα seen•doh•mah

soother [BE] πιπίλα
pee•pee•lah

sore throat πονόλαιμος
poh•noh•leh•mohs

sort n είδος ee•THohs; ν διαλέγω
THiah•leh•ghoh

south adj νότιος noh•tee•ohs

souvenir σουβενίρ soo•veh•neer

souvenir store κατάστημα
σουβενίρ kah•tahs•tee•mah
soo•veh•neer

spa σπα spah

space n (area) χώρος
khoh•rohs

spare (extra) επιπλέον
eh•peep•leh•ohn

speak μιλώ mee•loh

special requirement ειδική
ανάγκη ee•THee•kee
ah•nah•gkee

specialist ειδικός ee•THee•kohs

specimen δείγμα THeegh•mah

speed ν τρέχω treh•khoh

spend ξοδεύω ksoh•THeh•voh

spine σπονδυλική στήλη
spohn•THee•lee•kee stee•lee

spoon n κουτάλι koo•tah•lee

sport αθλητισμός
ahth•lee•teez•mohs

sporting goods store
κατάστημα αθλητικών
ειδών kah•tahs•tee•mah
ath•lee•tee•kohn ee•THohn

sports massage αθλητικό μασάζ
ahth•lee•tee•koh mah•sahz

sports stadium αθλητικό
στάδιο ahth•lee•tee•koh
stah•THee•oh

square τετράγωνος
teht•rah•ghoh•nohs

stadium στάδιο stah•THee•oh

stain n λεκές leh•kehs

stairs σκάλες skah•lehs

stale μπαγιάτικος
bah•yah•tee•kohs

stamp n (postage) γραμματόσημο
ghrah•mah•toh•see•moh

start ν αρχίζω ahr•khee•zoh

statement (legal) δήλωση
THee•loh•see

statue άγαλμα ah•ghahl•mah

stay ν μένω meh•noh

sterilizing solution
αποστειρωτικό διάλυμα
ah•pohs•tee•roh•tee•koh
THee•ah•lee•mah

sting n (insect) τσίμπημα
tsee•bee•mah

stolen κλεμένος kleh•meh•nohs

stomach n στομάχι
stoh•mah•khee

stomachache στομαχόπονος
stoh•mah•khoh•puh•nohs

stop n (bus) στάση stah•see; ν
σταματώ stah•mah•toh

store guide [BE] οδηγός
καταστήματος oh•THee•ghohs
kah•tahs•tee•mah•tohs

stove κουζίνα koo•zee•nah

straight ahead ευθεία
ehf•thee•ah

strange παράξενος
pah•rah•kseh•nohs

straw (drinking) καλαμάκι
kah•lah•mah•kee

stream n ρυάκι ree•ah•kee

street δρόμος THroh•mohs

string n (cord) σπάγγος spah•gohs

student φοιτητής fee•tee•tees

study ν σπουδάζω
spoo•THah•zoh

style n στυλ steel

subtitled με υπότιτλους meh
ee•poh•teet•loos

subway μετρό meht•roh

subway station σταθμός μετρό
stahth•mohs meh•troh

suggest προτείνω proh•tee•noh

suit (men's) κουστούμι
koos•too•mee; (women's)
ταγιέρ tah•yehr

suitable κατάλληλος
kah•tah•lee•lohs

sunburn n έγκαυμα ηλίου
ehn•gahv•mah ee•lee•oo

sunglasses γυαλιά ηλίου
yah•liah ee•lee•oo

sunshade [BE] ομπρέλλα
ohm•breh•lah

sunstroke ηλίαση ee•lee•ah•see

sun tan lotion λοσιόν
μαυρίσματος loh•siohn
mahv•rees•mah•tohs

sunscreen αντιηλιακό
ahn•dee•ee•lee•ah•koh

superb έξοχος eh•ksoh•khohs

supermarket σουπερμάρκετ
soo•pehr•mahr•keht

supervision επίβλεψη
eh•peev•leh•psee

surname επίθετο
eh•pee•theh•toh

sweatshirt φούτερ foo•tehr

swelling πρήξιμο pree•ksee•moh

swimming κολύμβηση
koh•leem•vee•see

swimming pool πισίνα
pee•see•nah

swimming trunks μαγιό
mah•yoh

swimsuit μαγιό mah•yoh

switch n διακόπτης
THiah•koh•ptees

swollen πρησμένος
preez•meh•nohs

symptom σύμπτωμα
seem•ptoh•mah

T

table τραπέζι trah•peh•zee

tablecloth τραπεζομάντηλο
trah•peh•zoh•mahn•dee•loh

tablet χάπι khah•pee

take παίρνω pehr•noh

take a photograph βγάζω
φωτογραφία vghah•zoh
foh•tohgh•rah•fee•ah

take away [BE] πακέτο για το
σπίτι pah•keh•toh yah toh
spee•tee

tall ψηλός psee•lohs

tampon ταμπόν tahm•bohn

tax n φόρος foh•rohs

taxi ταξί tah•ksee

taxi driver ταξιτζής
tah•ksee•jees

taxi rank [BE] πιάτσα ταξί
piah•tsah tah•ksee

teaspoon κουταλάκι
koo•tah•lah•kee

team n ομάδα oh•mah•THah

teenager έφηβος eh•fee•vohs

telephone n τηλέφωνο
tee•leh•foh•noh

telephone booth τηλεφωνικός
θάλαμος tee•leh•foh•nee•kohs
thah•lah•mohs

telephone call κλήση klee•see

telephone directory τηλεφωνικός
κατάλογος tee•leh•foh•
nee•kohs kah•tah•loh•ghohs

telephone number αριθμός
τηλεφώνου ah•reeth•mohs
tee•leh•foh•noo

tell λέω leh•oh

temperature (body) θερμοκρασία
theh•rmohk•rah•see•ah

temple ναός nah•ohs

temporary προσωρινός
proh•soh•ree•nohs

tennis τέννις teh•nees

tennis court γήπεδο τέννις
yee•peh•THah teh•nees

tent σκηνή skee•nee

terrible φοβερός foh•veh•rohs

theater θέατρο theh•aht•roh

theft κλοπή kloh•pee

there εκεί eh•kee

thermal bath ιαματικό λουτρό
ee•ah•mah•tee•koh loot•roh

thermos flask θερμός thehr•mohs

thick χοντρός khohn•drohs

thief κλέφτης klehf•tees

thin adj λεπτός lehp•tohs

think νομίζω noh•mee•zoh

thirsty διψάω THee•psah•oh

those εκείνα eh•kee•nah

throat λαιμός leh•mohs

thumb αντίχειρας
ahn•dee•khee•rahs

ticket εισιτήριο
ee•see•tee•ree•oh

ticket office γραφείο
εισιτηρίων ghrah•fee•oh
ee•see•tee•ree•ohn

tie n γραβάτα ghrah•vah•tah

tight adj στενός steh•nohs

tights [BE] n καλσόν kahl•sohn

timetable [BE] δρομολόγιο
THroh•moh•loh•yee•oh

tire λάστιχο lahs•tee•khoh

tired κουρασμένος
koo•rahz•meh•nohs

tissue χαρτομάντηλο
khahr•toh•mahn•dee•loh

toaster τοστιέρα toh•stieh•rah

tobacco καπνός kahp•nohs

tobacconist καπνοπωλείο
kahp•noh•poh•lee•oh

toilet [BE] τουαλέτα
too•ah•leh•tah

toilet paper χαρτί υγείας
khahr•tee ee•yee•ahs

toiletries καλλυντικά
kah•leen•dee•kah

tongue γλώσσα ghloh•sah

too (extreme) πάρα πολύ
pah•rah poh•lee

tooth δόντι THohn•dee

toothache πονόδοντος
poh•noh•THohn•dohs

toothbrush οδοντόβουρτσα
oh•THohn•doh•voor•tsah

toothpaste οδοντόπαστα
oh•THohn•doh•pahs•tah

top adj πάνω pah•noh

torn σχισμένος skheez•meh•nohs

tour guide ξεναγός
kseh•nah•ghohs

tourist τουρίστας too•rees•tahs

towards προς prohs

tower πύργος peer•ghohs

town πόλη poh•lee

town hall δημαρχείο
THee•mahr•khee•oh

toy store κατάστημα
παιχνιδιών kah•tahs•tee•mah
peh•khnee•THiohn

traditional παραδοσιακός
pah•rah•THoh•see•ah•kohs

traffic κίνηση kee•nee•see

trail μονοπάτι moh•noh•pah•tee

trailer τροχόσπιτο
troh•khohs•pee•toh

train τρένο treh•noh

train station σταθμός των
τρένων stahth•mohs tohn
treh•nohn

tram τραμ trahm

transfer μεταφέρω
meh•tah•feh•roh

transit n μεταφορά
meh•tah•foh•rah

translate μεταφράζω
meh•tah•frah•zoh

translation μετάφραση
meh•tah•frah•see

translator μεταφραστής
meh•tah•frah•stees

trash σκουπίδια *skoo•peeTH•yah*

trash can κάδος απορριμμάτων *kah•THohs ah•poh•ree•mah•tohn*

travel agency ταξιδιωτικό γραφείο *tah•ksee•THyoh• tee•koh ghrah•fee•oh*

travel sickness [BE] ναυτία *nahf•tee•ah*

traveler's check ταξιδιωτική επιταγή *tah•ksee•THee•oh• tee•kee ep•ee•tah•yee*

tray δίσκος *THees•kohs*

tree δέντρο *THehn•droh*

trim n διόρθωμα *THee•ohr•thoh•mah*

trolley [BE] (cart) καροτσάκι *kah•roh•tsah•kee*

trolley-bus τρόλλεϋ *troh•leh•ee*

trousers [BE] παντελόνι *pahn•deh•loh•nee*

try on δοκιμάζω *THoh•kee•mah•zoh*

T-shirt μπλουζάκι *bloo•zah•kee*

tunnel τούνελ *too•nehl*

turn v γυρίζω *yee•ree•zoh*

turn down v (volume, heat) χαμηλώνω *khah•mee•loh•noh*

turn off v σβήνω *svee•noh*

turn on v ανάβω *ah•nah•voh*

turn up v (volume, heat) ανεβάζω *ah•neh•vah•zoh*

TV τηλεόραση *tee•leh•oh•rah•see*

twin bed διπλό κρεβάτι *THeep•loh kreh•vah•tee*

typical τυπικός *tee•pee•kohs*

U

ugly άσχημος *ahs•khee•mohs*

unconscious αναίσθητος *ah•nehs•thee•tohs*

underground [BE] υπόγειος *ee•poh•ghee•ohs*

underpants [BE] κυλοτάκι *kee•loh•tah•kee*

understand καταλαβαίνω *kah•tah•lah•veh•noh*

uneven (ground) ανώμαλος *ah•noh•mah•lohs*

unfortunately δυστυχώς *THees•tee•khohs*

uniform n στολή *stoh•lee*

unique μοναδικός *moh•nah•THee•kohs*

unit μονάδα *moh•nah•THah*

United Kingdom Ηνωμένο Βασίλειο *ee•noh•meh•noh vah•see•lee•oh*

United States Ηνωμένες Πολιτείες *ee•noh•meh•nehs poh•lee•tee•es*

university Πανεπιστήμιο *pah•neh•pees•tee•mee•oh*

unlimited mileage απεριόριστα χιλιόμετρα *ah•peh•ree•ohr•ees•tah khee•lioh•meht•rah*

unpleasant δυσάρεστος *THee•sah•reh•stohs*

upper (berth) πάνω (κουκέτα) *pah•noh (koo•keh•tah)*

upstairs επάνω *eh•pah•noh*

urgent επείγον *eh•pee•ghohn*

use v χρησιμοποιώ *khree•see•moh•pee•oh*

useful χρήσιμος *khree•see•mohs*

V

vacancy ελεύθερο δωμάτιο *eh•lehf•theh•roh THoh•mah•tee•oh*

vacant ελεύθερος *eh•lehf•theh•rohs*

vacation διακοπές *THee•ah•koh•pehs*

vacation resort θέρετρο διακοπών *theh•reh•troh THee•ah•koh•pohn*

vaccination εμβόλιο *ehm•voh•lee•oh*

valid ισχύει *ee•skhee•ee*

valley κοιλάδα *kee•lah•THah*

valuable πολύτιμος *poh•lee•tee•mohs*

value n αξία *ah•ksee•ah*

VAT [BE] ΦΠΑ *fee•pee•ah*

vegetarian χορτοφάγος *khohr•toh•fah•ghohs*

vein φλέβα *fleh•vah*

velvet βελούδο *veh•loo•THoh*

very πολύ *poh•lee*

video βιντεοκασέτα *vee•deh•oh•kah•seh•tah*

video game παιχνίδι βίντεο *pehkh•nee•THee vee•deh•oh*

village χωριό *khohr•yoh*

visa βίζα *vee•zah*

visit n επίσκεψη *eh•pees•keh•psee*

volleyball βόλεϋ *voh•leh•ee*

vomit v εμετό *kah•noh eh•meh•toh*

W

wait v περιμένω *peh•ree•meh•noh*

waiter n υγκαροόν *gahr•sohn*

waitress δεσποινίς *THehs•pee•nees*

wake v ξυπνώ *ksee•pnoh*

walk v περπατώ *peh•pah•toh*

walking route διαδρομή περιήγησης *THee•ah•THroh•mee peh•ree•ee•ye•sees*

wall τοίχος *tee•khohs*

wallet πορτοφόλι *pohr•toh•foh•lee*

want θέλω *theh•loh*

warm ζεστός *zehs•tohs*

washing machine πλυντήριο *pleen•tee•ree•oh*

watch n ρολόι *roh•loh•ee*

watch strap λουρί ρολογιού *loo•ree roh•loh•yioo*

water n νερό *neh•roh*

waterfall καταρράχτης *kah•tah•rahkh•tees*

waterproof αδιάβροχος
ah•THee•ah•vroh•khohs
wave *n* κύμα *kee•mah*
way δρόμος *THroh•mohs*
wear *v* φορώ *foh•roh*
weather καιρός *keh•rohs*
weather forecast πρόβλεψη
καιρού *prohv•leh•psee keh•roo*
wedding γάμος *ghah•mohs*
west δυτικά *THee•tee•kah*
wetsuit στολή δύτη *stoh•lee•
THee•tee*
wheelchair αναπηρική
καρέκλα *ah•nah•pee•ree•kee
kah•rehk•lah*
wide φαρδύς *fahr•THees*
wife σύζυγος *see•zee•ghohs*
window παράθυρο
pah•rah•thee•roh

window seat θέση δίπλα στο
παράθυρο *theh•see THeep•lah
stoh pah•rah•thee•roh*
winery οινοποιείο
ee•noh•pee•ee•oh
wireless internet ασύρματο
ίντερνετ *ah•see•rmah•toh
ee•nteh•rnet*
with με *meh*
withdraw κάνω ανάληψη
kah•noh ah•nah•lee•psee
without χωρίς *khoh•rees*
witness μάρτυρας *mahr•tee•rahs*
wood (forest) δάσος *THah•sohs;*
(material) ξύλο *ksee•loh*
work δουλειώ *THoo•lee•voh*
worry ανησυχώ *ah•nee•see•khoh*
worse χειρότερος
khee•roh•teh•rohs

wound (cut) πληγή *plee•yee*
write (down) γράφω *ghrah•foh*
wrong λάθος *lah•thohs*

X

x-ray ακτινογραφία
ahk•tee•nohgh•rah•fee•ah

Y

yacht γιωτ *yoht*
yellow κίτρινος *keet•ree•nohs*
young νέος *neh•ohs*
youth hostel ξενώνας
νεότητας *kseh•noh•nahs
neh•oh•tee•tahs*

Z

zoo ζωολογικός κήπος
zoh•oh•loh•yee•kohs kee•pohs

A

ATM *ehee•tee•ehm* ATM
άγαλμα *ah•ghahl•mah* statue
αγαπημένος *ah•ghah•pee•
meh* favorite
αγαπώ *ah•ghah•poh* v love
αγγειοπλαστική *ahn•gee•ohp•
lahs•tee•kee* pottery
Αγγλία *ahng•lee•ah* England
αγγλικά *ahng•lee•kah* English
language
αγγλικός *ahng•lee•kohs* adj
English
Άγγλος *ahng•lohs* English
(nationality)
αγενής *ah•yeh•nees* rude
αγορά *ah•ghoh•rah* n market
αγοράζω *ah•ghoh•rah•zoh* buy
αγόρι *ah•ghoh•ree* boy
αγώνας *ah•ghoh•nahs* n match
(sport)

άδεια *ah•THee•ah* n permit
άδεια σκι *ah•THee•ah skee*
lift pass
άδειος *ahTH•yohs* adj empty
αδιάβροχο *ah•THee•
ahv•oh•khoh* raincoat
αδιάβροχος *ah•THee•ahv•
roh•khohs* waterproof
αδύναμος *ah•THee•nah•mohs*
weak
αεροδρόμιο *ah•eh•roh•
THroh•mee•oh* airport
αεροπλάνο *ah•eh•rohp•lah•noh*
n plane
αεροπορική εταιρία
*ah•eh•roh•poh•ree•kee
eh•teh•ree•ah* airline
αεροπορικώς *ah•eh•roh•
poh•ree•kohs* airmail
αηδιαστικός *ah•ee•THee•ah•
stee•kohs* revolting

αθλητικά παπούτσια *ath•lee•
tee•kah pah•poo•tsiah*
sneakers
αθλητικό στάδιο *ahth•lee•
tee•koh stah•THee•oh* sports
stadium
αθλητικός όμιλος
*ahth•lee•tee•kohs
oh•mee•lohs* sports club
αθλητισμός *ahth•lee•teez•mohs*
sport
αθώος *ah•thoh•ohs* innocent
αιμορραγία *eh•moh•rah•yee•ah*
n bleed
αιμορραγώ *eh•moh•rah•yoh*
v bleed
αίθουσα συναυλιών
eh•thoo•sah see•nahv•lee•ohn
concert hall
ακολουθώ *ah•koh•loo•thoh*
v follow

ακουστικό βαρυκοΐας ah•koo•
stee•_koh_ vah•ree•koh•ee•ahs
hearing aid

ακριβός ahk•ree•_vohs_ expensive

ακτή ahk•_tee_ n shore

ακτινογραφία ahk•tee•
nohgh•rah•_fee_•ah x-ray

ακυρώνω ah•kee•_roh_•oh
v cancel

αληθινός ah•lee•thee•_nohs_ real
(genuine)

αλλά ah•_lah_ conj but

άλλα ah•lah others

αλλαγή ah•lah•_yee_ n change

αλλάζω ah•_lah_•zoh v exchange
(money)

αλλεργικός ahl•ehr•yee•_kohs_
allergic

αλληλογραφία ah•lee•lohgh•
rah•_fee_•ah n mail

άλλο ένα _ah_•loh eh•nah extra
(additional)

άλλος _ah_•lohs another

αλουμινόχαρτο ah•loo•mee•
noh•khah•rtoh aluminum foil

Αμερικανός ah•mee•ree•
kah•_nohs_ n American

αμέσως ah•_meh_•sohs immediately

άμμος _ah_•mohs sand

ανάβω ah•_nah_•voh v turn on

αναίσθητος ah•_nehs_•thee•tohs
unconscious

ανάκτορα ah•_nahk_•toh•rah
palace

αναλυτικός λογαριασμός
ah•nah•lee•tee•_kohs_ loh•
ghahr•yahz•_mohs_ itemized bill

αναπηρική καρέκλα
ah•nah•pee•ree•_kee_
kah•_rehk_•lah wheelchair

αναπνευστήρας ah•nahp•
nehf•_stee_•rahs snorkel

αναπνέω ah•nahp•_neh_•oh v breathe

αναπτήρας ah•nahp•_tee_•rahs n
lighter (cigarette)

αναρρίχηση ah•nah•_ree_•
khee•see rock climbing

ανατολικά ah•nah•toh•lee•_kah_
east

αναφέρω ah•nah•_feh_•roh
mention (report)

αναχώρηση ah•nah•_khoh_•
ree•see departure (travel)

άνδρας _ahn_•THrahs n male
(man)

ανεμιστήρας ah•neh•mees•
tee•rahs n fan (air)

ανεβάζω ah•neh•_vah_•zoh v turn
up (volume, heat)

ανέκδοτο ah•_nehk_•THoh•toh
n joke

ανησυχώ ah•nee•see•_khoh_
worry

ανθοπωλείο ahn•thoh•poh•
lee•oh florist

ανοίγω ah•_nee_•ghoh v open

ανοιχτήρι ah•neekh•_tee_•ree
can opener

ανοιχτός ah•neekh•_tohs_ adj light
(color), open

ανοιχτότερος
ah•neekh•_toh_•teh•rohs adj
lighter (color)

ανταλλακτικό ahn•dah•
lahk•tee•_koh_ replacement part

αντιβιοτικό ahn•dee•
vee•oh•tee•_koh_ antibiotic

αντιηλιακό ahn•dee•
lee•ah•_koh_ sunscreen

αντισηπτική κρέμα
ahn•dee•seep•tee•_kee_
kreh•mah antiseptic cream

αντίχειρας ahn•_dee_•khee•rahs
thumb

ανώμαλος ah•_noh_•mah•lohs
uneven (ground)

αξεσουάρ ah•kseh•soo•_ahr_
accessory

αξία ah•_ksee_•ah n value

αξιοθέατο ah•ksee•oh•
theh•ah•tah sightseeing sight

απαγορευμένος ah•pah•ghoh•
rehv•_meh_•nohs prohibited

απαραίτητος ah•pah•_reh_•
tee•tohs essential, necessary

απασχολημένος ah•pahs•
khoh•lee•_meh_•nohs adj busy
(occupied)

απέναντι ah•_peh_•nahn•dee
opposite

απεριόριστα χιλιόμετρα
ah•peh•ree•_ohr_•ees•tah khee•
lioh•meht•rah unlimited mileage

απλό εισιτήριο ahp•_loh_
ee•see•_tee_•ree•oh one-way
(single BE) ticket

απλός ahp•_lohs_ simple

από ah•_poh_ from

απομίμηση ah•poh•_mee_•
mee•see imitation

αποβάθρα ah•poh•_vahth_•rah
platform, quay

απόγευμα ah•_poh_•yehv•mah
afternoon

απόδειξη ah•_poh_•THee•ksee
receipt

απορρυπαντικό ah•poh•
ree•pahn•dee•_koh_ detergent

αποσμητικό ah•pohz•
mee•tee•_koh_ deodorant

αποσκευές ah•pohs•keh•_vehs_
baggage [BE]

αποσκευές χειρός ah•pohs•
keh•vehs khee•_rohs_ hand
luggage

αποστειρωτικό διάλυμα
ah•pohs•tee•roh•tee•_koh_ THee•
_ah_•lee•mah sterilizing solution

απόχρωση ah•_pohkh_•roh•see
shade (color)

απώλεια ah•_poh_•lee•ah n loss

αργά ahr•_ghah_ adv late

αργία ahr•_yee_•ah public holiday

αργός ahr•_ghohs_ adj slow

αριθμός κυκλοφορίας
ah•reeth•_mohs_ kee•kloh•
foh•_ree_•ahs registration number

αριθμός πτήσεως *ah•reeth•mohs ptee•seh•ohs* flight number

αριθμός τηλεφώνου *ah•reeth•mohs tee•leh•foh•noo* telephone number

αριστερός *ah•rees•teh•rohs* left *(adj)*

αριστερά *ah•rees•teh•rah* left *(adv)*

αρκετά *ahr•keh•tah* enough

αρραβωνιαστικιά *ah•rah•voh•niahs•tee•kiah* fiancée

αρραβωνιαστικός *ah•rah•voh•niahs•tee•kohs* fiancé

αρρώστεια *ahr•ohs•tee•ah* illness

άρρωστος *ah•rohs•tohs* adj sick

αρτοποιείο *ah•rtoh•pee•ee•oh* bakery

αρχάριος *ah•khah•ree•ohs* beginner

αρχίζω v *ah•khee•zoh* start

ασανσέρ *ah•sahn•sehr* n lift (elevator)

ασήμι *ah•see•mee* silver

ασύρματο ίντερνετ *ah•see•rmah•toh ee•nteh•rnet* wireless internet

ασθενοφόρο *ahs•theh•noh•foh•roh* ambulance

ασθματικός *ahsth•mah•tee•kohs* asthmatic

ασπιρίνη *ahs•pee•ree•nee* aspirin

αστυνομία *ah•stee•noh•mee•ah* n police

αστυνομικό τμήμα *ah•stee•noh•mee•koh tmee•mah* police station

ασφάλεια *ah•fah•lee•ah* n fuse; insurance

ασφάλεια αποζημίωσης *ahs•fah•lee•ah ah•poh•zee•mee•oh•sees* insurance claim

ασφάλεια υγείας *ahs•fah•lee•ah ee•yee•ahs* health insurance

ασφαλής *ahs•fah•lees* adj safe (not dangerous)

ασφαλιστική εταιρία *ahs•fah•lees•tee•kee eh•teh•ree•ah* insurance company

άσχημος *ahs•khee•mohs* ugly

άτομο με ειδικές ανάγκες *ah•toh•moh meh eh•THee•kehs ah•nahn•gehs* disabled

ατύχημα *ah•tee•khee•mah* accident

αυθεντικός *ahf•thehn•dee•kohs* genuine

αυθεντικότητα *ahf•thehn•dee•koh•tee•tah* authenticity

αϋπνία *ah•ee•pnee•ah* insomnia

αυτοκίνητο *ahf•toh•kee•nee•toh* car

αυχένας *ahf•kheh•nahs* neck (part of body)

αφήνω *ah•fee•noh* v leave (let go)

αφορολόγητα είδη *ah•foh•roh•loh•yee•tah ee•THee* duty-free goods

αφρόλουτρο για ντους *ahf•roh•loot•roh yah dooz* shower gel

αχθοφόρος *ahkh•thoh•foh•rohs* porter

Β

βαμβάκι *vahm•vah•kee* cotton

βαγκόν-λι *vah•gohn•lee* sleeping car

βάζο *vah•zoh* n jar

βάζω *vah•zoh* v put

βαλές *vah•lehs* jack

βαρετός *vah•reh•tohs* boring

βάρκα *vahr•kah* boat

βαρύς *vah•rees* heavy

βασιλιάς *vah•see•liahs* king

βγαίνω *vyeh•noh* get out (of vehicle)

βελούδο *veh•loo•THoh* velvet

βενζινάδικο *vehn•zee•nah•THee•koh* gas (petrol BE) station

βενζίνη *vehn•zee•nee* gasoline (petrol BE)

βερνίκι παπουτσιών *vehr•nee•kee pah•poo•tsiohn* shoe polish

βήχας *vee•khahs* n cough

βήχω *vee•khoh* v cough

βιβλίο *veev•lee•oh* n book

βιβλιοθήκη *veev•lee•oh•thee•kee* library

βιβλιοπωλείο *veev•lee•oh•poh•lee•oh* bookstore

βίδα *vee•THah* n screw

βίζα *vee•zah* visa

βιντεοκασέτα *vee•deh•oh•kah•seh•tah* video

βλάβη *vlah•vee* breakdown n (car)

βλέπω *vleh•poh* v see

βοήθεια *voh•ee•thee•ah* n help

βοηθώ *voh•ee•thoh* v help

βόλεϊ *voh•leh•ee* volleyball

βόρεια *voh•ree•ah* north

βοτανικός κήπος *voh•tah•nee•kohs kee•pohs* botanical garden

βουνό *voo•noh* mountain

βουρτσίζω *voor•tsee•zoh* v brush

βραδινό *vrah•THee•noh* dinner

βράδυ *vrah•THee* evening

βράζω *vrah•zoh* boil

βράχος *vrah•khohs* n rock

βρετανικός *vreh•tah•nee•kohs* British adj

Βρετανός *vreh•tah•nohs* British (nationality)

βρέχει *vreh•khee* v rain

βροχή *vroh•khee* n rain

βρύση *vree•see* faucet

βρώμικος *vroh•mee•kohs* adj dirty

Γ

γάμος *ghah•mohs* wedding

γάζα *ghah•zah* bandage

γαλάκτωμα για τα μαλλιά *ghah•lah•ktoh•mah yah tah mah•liah* conditioner (hair)

γάντι *ghahn•dee* n glove

γαστρίτιδα _ghahs•tree•tee•THah_ gastritis

γεμάτος _yeh•mah_ adj full

γείτονας _yee•toh•nahs_ n neighbor

γελώ _yeh•loh_ v laugh

γεμιστή _yeh•mees•tee_ stuffed olive

γέρικος _yeh•ree•kohs_ old (person)

γεύμα _yehv•mah_ meal

γέφυρα _yeh•fee•rah_ n bridge (over water)

γη _ghee_ n land

γήπεδο γκολφ _yee•peh•THoh gohlf_ golf course

γήπεδο τέννις _yee•peh•THoh teh•nees_ tennis court

γιατρός _yah•trohs_ doctor

γιωτ _yoht_ yacht

γκαράζ _gah•rahz_ garage

γκαρσόν _gahr•sohn_ waiter

γκολφ _gohlf_ golf

γκρουπ _groop_ n group

γλώσσα _ghloh•sah_ tongue

γνωρίζω _ghnoh•ree•zoh_ know

γόνατο _ghoh•nah•toh_ knee

γονείς _ghoh•nees_ parents

γράμμα _ghrah•mah_ letter

γραμματόσημο _ghrah•mah•toh•see•moh_ n stamp (postage)

γραμμή _ghrah•mee_ n line (subway)

γραβάτα _ghrah•vah•tah_ n tie

γρασίδι _ghrah•see•THee_ grass

γραφείο _ghrah•fee•oh_ office

γραφείο ανταλλαγής συναλλάγματος _ghrah•fee•oh ahn•dah•lah•yees see•nah•lahgh•mah•tohs_ currency exchange office

γραφείο εισιτηρίων _ghrah•fee•oh ee•see•tee•ree•ohn_ ticket office

γραφείο πληροφοριών _ghrah•fee•oh plee•roh•foh•ree•ohn_ information office

γράφω _ghrah•foh_ write (down)

γρήγορα _ghree•ghoh•rah_ adv fast

γρήγορος _ghree•ghoh•rohs_ quick

γρίππη _ghree•pee_ flu

γυαλιά _yiah•liah_ glasses (optical)

γυαλιά ηλίου _yah•liah ee•lee•oo_ sun glasses

γυναικολόγος _yee•neh•koh•loh•ghohs_ gynecologist

γυρίζω _yee•ree•zoh_ v turn

γωνία _ghoh•nee•ah_ corner

Δ

δανείζω _THah•nee•zoh_ lend

δάσος _THah•sohs_ n forest (wood)

δάχτυλο _THah•tee•loh_ n finger

δείγμα _THeegh•mah_ specimen

δείχνω _THeekh•noh_ v point (show)

δέντρο _THehn•droh_ tree

δεξιός _THeh•ksee•ohs_ adj right (not left)

δέρμα _THehr•mah_ n skin

δημαρχείο _THee•mahr•khee•oh_ town hall

δημοφιλής _THee•moh•fee•lees_ popular

δηλητήριο _THee•lee•tee•ree•oh_ n poison

δηλητηριώδης _THee•lee•tee•ree•oh•THees_ poisonous

δηλώνω _THee•loh•noh_ declare

δήλωση _THee•loh•see_ statement (legal)

δημόσιος _THee•moh•see•ohs_ public

διαμάντι _THiah•mahn•dee_ n diamond

διαμέρισμα _THee•ah•meh•reez•mah_ apartment

διάβαση πεζών _THee•ah•vah•see peh•zohn_ pedestrian crossing

διαβατήριο _THiah•vah•tee•ree•oh_ passport

διαβητικός _THee•ah•vee•tee•kohs_ diabetic

διαδρομή _THee•ahTH•roh•mee_ n route

διάδρομος _THee•ah•THroh•mohs_ aisle seat

διαζευγμένος _THee•ah•zehv•ghmeh•nohs_ divorced

διακοπές _THee•ah•koh•pehs_ vacation (holiday BE)

διακόπτης _THiah•koh•ptees_ n switch

διαμέρισμα _THee•ah•mehr•ees•mah_ n flat

διάρροια _THee•ah•ree•ah_ diarrhea

διάσημος _THee•ah•see•mohs_ famous

διεθνής _THee•eth•nees_ international

διεθνής φοιτητική κάρτα _THee•ehth•nees fee•tee•tee•kee kahr•tah_ International Student Card

διερμηνέας _THee•ehr•mee•neh•ahs_ interpreter

διεύθυνση _THee•ehf•theen•see_ n address

διευθυντής _THee•ehf•theen•dees_ manager

δικηγόρος _THee•kee•ghoh•rohs_ lawyer

δίκλινο δωμάτιο _THeek•lee•noh THoh•mah•tee•oh_ double room

δίνω _THee•noh_ give

διόρθωμα _THee•ohr•thoh•mah_ n trim

δίπλα _THeep•lah_ next to

διπλό κρεβάτι _THeep•loh kreh•vah•tee_ twin bed

δίσκος _THees•kohs_ tray

διψάω _THee•psah•oh_ thirsty

δοκιμάζω _THoh•kee•mah•zoh_

try on

δολάριο THoh•_lah_•ree•oh dollar

δόντι THohn•dee tooth

δοσολογία THoh•soh•loh•_yee_•ah dosage

δουλειά THoo•_liah_ job

δουλεύω THoo•_leh_•voh work

δρομολόγιο THroh•moh•_loh_•yee•oh time table

δρόμος THroh•mohs road, street, way

δυνατός THee•nah•_tohs_ adj loud

δυσάρεστος THee•_sah_•reh stohs unpleasant

δύσκολος THee•skoh•lohs difficult

δυσπεψία THes•peh•_psee_•ah indigestion

δυστυχώς THees•tee•_khohs_ unfortunately

δυτικά THee•tee•_kah_ west

δωμάτιο THoh•_mah_•tee•oh n room

δώρο THoh•roh gift

E

ελιά eh•_liah_ olive

εμβόλιο ehm•_voh_•lee•oh vaccination

εμπορικό κέντρο ehm•boh•ree•_koh_ _keh_•ntroh shopping mall [centre BE]

εγγύηση eh•_gee_•ee•see n guarantee

εγγυώμαι eh•gee•oh•_meh_ v guarantee

έγκαυμα ηλίου _ehn_•gahv•mah ee•_lee_•oo n sun burn

έγκυος eh•_gee_•ohs pregnant

έδαφος eh•THah•fohs ground (earth)

εδώ eh•_THoh_ here

εδώ κοντά eh•_THoh_ kohn•_dah_ nearby

εθνική οδός ehth•nee•_kee_ ee

oh•_THohs_ highway, motorway

εθνικός eth•nee•_kohs_ national

εθνικός δρυμός eth•nee•_kohs_ THree•_mohs_ nature reserve

είμαι ee•_meh_ be

είμαι κουφός koo•_fohs_ deaf

είδη οικιακής χρήσεως _ee_•THee•ee•kee•ah•_kees_ khree•seh•ohs household articles

ειδική ανάγκη ee•THee•_kee_ ah•_nahn_•gkee special requirement

ειδικός ee•THee•_kohs_ specialist

είδος ee•THohs kind (sort)

εισιτήριο ee•see•_tee_•ree•oh fare (ticket)

εισιτήριο με επιστροφή ee•see•_tee_•ree•oh meh eh•pee•stroh•_fee_ roundtrip [return BE] ticket

εκδρομή ehk•THroh•_mee_ excursion

εκεί eh•_kee_ there, over there

εκείνα eh•_kee_•nah those

έκθεση _ehk_•theh•see exhibition

έκπτωση _ehk_•ptoh•see reduction

έκτακτη ανάγκη _ehk_•tahk•tee ah•_nah_•gee emergency

ελάχιστος eh•_lah_•khees•tohs minimum

ελεύθερο δωμάτιο eh•_lehf_•theh•roh THoh•_mah_•tee•oh vacancy

ελεύθερος eh•_lehf_•theh•rohs adj free, single, vacant

ελικόπτερο eh•lee•_kohp_•teh•roh helicopter

Ελλάδα eh•_lah_•THah Greece

Έλληνας eh•lee•nahs Greek (nationality)

ελληνικός eh•lee•nee•_kohs_ adj Greek

ένα βράδυ eh•nah vrah•THee

overnight

ένα τέταρτο eh•nah teh•tah•rtoh quarter (quantity)

ενδιαφέρων en•THee•ah•_feh_•rohn interesting

ένεση eh•neh•see injection

ενήλικας eh•_nee_•lee•kahs adult

ενοχλώ eh•noh•_khloh_ disturb

έντομο _ehn_•doh•moh insect

εντομοαπωθητικό ehn•doh•moh•ah•poh•thee•tee•_koh_ insect repellent

έντυπο _ehn_•dee•poh n form

εντυπωσιακός ehn•dee•poh•see•ah•_kohs_ impressive

ενυδατική κρέμα eh•nee•THah•tee•_kee_ _kreh_•mah moisturizer (cream)

εξάνθημα eh•_ksahn_•thee•mah n rash

εξαργυρώνω eh•ksahr•ghee•_roh_•noh v cash

εξόγκωμα eh•_ksoh_•goh•mah n lump (medical)

έξοδος eh•ksoh•THohs n gate (airport); exit

έξοδος κινδύνου eh•ksoh•THohs keen•_THee_•noo emergency, fire exit

εξοχή eh•ksoh•_khee_ countryside

έξοχος eh•ksoh•khohs superb

εξπρές ehk•_sprehs_ express (mail)

εξυπηρέτηση eh•ksee•pee•_reh_•tee•see facility

έξω eh•ksoh adv out

έξω eh•ksoh adj outside

εξωλέμβιο eh•ksoh•_lehm_•vee•oh motorboat

εξωτερικός eh•ksoh•teh•ree•_kohs_ outdoor

επαναλαμβάνω eh•pah•nah•lahm•_vah_•noh v repeat

επάνω eh•_pah_•noh upstairs

επείγον eh•_ghohn_ urgent

επιμένω eh•pee•_meh_•noh insist

επιβάτης eh•pee•_vah_•tees

passenger

επιβεβαιώνω eh•pee•veh•veh•_oh_•noh confirm

επίβλεψη eh•_peev_•leh•psee supervision

επίθεση eh•_pee_•theh•see n attack

επίθετο eh•_pee_•theh•toh surname

επικοινωνώ eh•pee•kee•noh•_noh_ v contact

επιληπτικός eh•pee•leep•tee•_kohs_ epileptic

επίπεδο eh•_pee_•peh•THoh level (even)

επίπεδος eh•_pee_•peh•THohs adj flat

έπιπλα eh•_peep_•lah furniture

επιπλέον eh•pee•_pleh_•oh spare (extra)

επισκευάζω eh•pee•skeh•_vah_•zoh v repair

επισκευή eh•pee•skeh•_vee_ n repair

επισκευή παπουτσιών eh•pee•skeh•_vee_ pah•poo•_tsiohn_ shoe repair

επίσκεψη eh•_pees_•keh•psee n visit

επιστροφή χρημάτων eh•pees•troh•_fee_ khree•_mah_•tohn n refund

επιταγή eh•pee•tah•_yee_ n check [cheque BE] (bank)

επιτίθεμαι eh•pee•_tee_•theh•meh v attack

επιτόκιο eh•pee•_toh_•kee•oh interest rate

επόμενος eh•_poh_•meh•nohs next

έρχομαι ehr•_khoh_•meh come

ερώτηση eh•_roh_•tee•see n question

εστιατόριο ehs•tee•ah•_toh_•ree•oh restaurant

εσωτερική γραμμή eh•soh•teh•ree•_kee_

ghrah•_mee_ extension (number)

εσωτερική πισίνα eh•soh•teh•ree•_kee_ pee•_see_•nah indoor pool

εσωτερικός eh•soh•teh•ree•_kohs_ indoor

ετικέτα eh•tee•_keh_•tah n label

έτοιμος eh•tee•mohs adj ready

ευθεία ehf•_thee_•ah straight ahead

εύκολος _ehf_•koh•lohs adj easy

ευρώ ehv•_roh_ euro

Ευρωπαϊκή Ένωση ehv•roh•pah•ee•_kee_ eh•noh•see European Union

ευτυχώς ehf•tee•_khohs_ fortunately

ευχαριστιέμαι ehf•khah•rees•_tieh_•meh enjoy

ευχάριστος ehf•_khah_•rees•tohs pleasant

εφημερίδα eh•fee•mehree•_THah_ newspaper

έφηβος _eh_•khoh•vohs teenager

έχω _eh_•khoh have (possession)

Ζ

ζαχαροπλαστείο zah•khah•rohp•lahs•_tee_•oh pastry store

ζεστός zes•_tohs_ hot, warm (weather)

ζημιά zee•_miah_ n damage

ζητώ zee•_toh_ ask

ζωγραφίζω zohgh•rah•_fee_•zoh v paint

ζωγράφος zohgh•_rah_•fohs painter

ζώνη _zoh_•nee belt

ζώνη για χρήματα _zoh_•nee yah _khree_•mah•tah money-belt

Η

ημερομηνία λήξεως ee•meh•roh•mee•_nee_•ah _lee_•kseh•ohs expiration date

ημερολόγιο ee•meh•roh•

loh•yee•oh calendar

ημικρανία ee•mee•krah•_nee_•ah migraine

ηλεκτρικός ee•lehk•tree•_kohs_ electric

ηλεκτρονικό εισιτήριο ee•leh•ktroh•nee•_koh_ ee•see•_tee_•ree•oh e-ticket

ηλεκτρονικό ταχυδρομείο ee•lehk•troh•nee•_koh_ tah•hee•dro•_mee_•oh (lee•meh•eel) e-mail

ηλεκτροπληξία ee•leh•ktroh•plee•_ksee_•ah shock (electric)

ηλίαση ee•_lee_•ah•see sun stroke

ηλικιωμένος ee•lee•kee•oh•_meh_•nohs senior citizen

Ηνωμένες Πολιτείες ee•noh•_meh_•nehs poh•lee•_tee_•ehs United States

Ηνωμένο Βασίλειο ee•noh•_meh_•noh vah•_see_•lee•oh United Kingdom

ηρεμιστικό ee•reh•mee•stee•_koh_ sedative

ήσυχος _ee_•see•khohs adj quiet

Θ

θάλασσα _thah_•lah•sah sea

θέατρο _theh_•aht•roh theater

θέλω _theh_•loh want

θέρμανση _thehr_•mahn•see heating

θερμή πηγή thehr•_mee_ pee•_yee_ hot spring

θερμόμετρο thehr•_moh_•meht•roh thermometer

θερμοκρασία thehr•mohk•rah•_see_•ah temperature (body)

θερμός thehr•_mohs_ thermos flask

θέρετρο διακοπών _theh_•reh•troh THee•ah•koh•_pohn_ vacation resort

θέση _theh_•see n location (space), seat

θέση δίπλα στο παράθυρο
theh•see THeee•_lah_ stoh
pah•_rah_•thee•roh window seat
θηλυκός thee•lee•_kohs_ female
θορυβώδης thoh•ree•_voh_•THees
noisy
θρησκεία three•_skee_•ah religion
θυμάμαι thee•_mah_•meh
remember
θυρίδα thee•_ree_•THah luggage
locker (lock-up)

Ι

ιατρική εξέταση ee•ah•tree•
kee eh•_kseh_•tah•see examination (medical)
ίδιος _ee_•THee•ohs same
ιδιωτικό μπάνιο
ee•THee•oh•tee•_koh bah_•nioh
private bathroom
ιερέας ee•eh•_reh_•ahs priest
ινσουλίνη een•soo•_lee_•nee
insulin
ίντερνετ _ee_•nteh•rnet internet
ίντερνετ καφέ _ee_•nteh•rnet
kah•_feh_ internet cafe
ιπποδρομία
ee•poh•THroh•_mee_•ah horse
racing
ιστιοπλοϊκό ees•tee•oh•
ploh•ee•_koh_ sailing boat
ιστορία ee•stoh•_ree_•ah history
ισχύει ee•_skhee_•ee valid
ίσως _ee_•sohs maybe, perhaps
ιώδειο ee•_oh_•THee•oh iodine

Κ

κάδος απορριμμάτων
kah•THohs ah•poh•ree•
mah•tohn trash can
καθαρισμός προσώπου
kah•thah•reez•_mohs_
proh•_soh_•poo facial
καθαρός kah•thah•_rohs_ clean
καθαρτικό kah•thahr•tee•_koh_
laxative

καθεδρικός ναός kah•theh•
THree•_kohs_ nah•_ohs_ cathedral
καθήκον kah•_thee_•kohn duty
(obligation)
κάθομαι _kah_•thoh•meh sit
καθρέφτης kah•_threhf_•tees
n mirror
καθυστέρηση kah•thee•
steh•ree•see n delay
καθυστερώ kah•thee•steh•_roh_
v delay
καινούργιος keh•_noor_•yohs new
καιρός keh•_rohs_ weather
καλά kah•_lah_ adv fine (well)
καλαμάκι kah•lah•_mah_•kee
straw (drinking)
καλάθι kah•_lah_•THee basket
καλός kah•_lohs_ good
καλσόν kah•_sohn_ n tights
κάλτσες _kahl_•tsehs socks
κάλυμμα φακού _kah_•lee•mah
fah•_koo_ lens cap
καλώ kah•_loh_ v call
κάμπινγκ _kah_•mpeeng camping
καναπές kah•nah•_pehs_ sofa
κανένας kah•_neh_•nahs adj none
κάνω ανάληψη _kah_•noh
ah•_nah_•lee•psee withdraw
κάνω εμετό _kah_•noh
eh•meh•_toh_ v vomit
κάνω κράτηση _kah_•noh
krah•tee•see v book
κάνω πεζοπορία _kah_•noh
peh•zoh•poh•_ree_•ah v hike
καπέλο kah•_peh_•loh hat
καπνίζω kahp•_nee_•zoh v smoke
καπνοπωλείο kahp•noh•
poh•_lee_•oh tobacconist
καπνός kahp•_nohs_ tobacco
καραντίνα kah•rahn•_dee_•nah n
quarantine
καράφα kah•_rah_•fah carafe
καρδιά kahr•_THee•ah_ v heart
καρδιακό έμφραγμα
kahr•THee•ah•_koh_
ehm•frahgh•mah heart attack

καροτσάκι kah•roh•_tsah_•kee
trolley (cart)
καροτσάκια αποσκευών
kah•roh•tsah•kiah
ah•pohs•keh•vohn baggage
[BE] carts (trolleys)
κάρτα-κλειδί _kahr_•tah klee•_dee_
key card
καρτποστάλ kahrt•poh•_stahl_
post card
κασκόλ kahs•_kohl_ scarf
κασσίτερος kah•_see_•teh•rohs
pewter
κάστρο _kahs_•troh castle
καταδυτικός εξοπλισμός kah•
tah•THee•tee•_kohs_ eh•ksoh•
pleez•mohs diving equipment
καταλαβαίνω kah•tah•lah•
veh•noh understand
κατάλληλος kah•_tah_•lee•lohs
suitable
καταρράχτης
kah•tah•_rahkh_•tees waterfall
κατάστημα kah•_tah_•stee•mah
shop (store)
κατάστημα με αντίκες
kah•_tah_•stee•mah meh
ahn•_tee_•kehs antiques store
κατάστημα με είδη δώρων
kah•_tah_•stee•mah meh
ee•THee THoh•rohn gift store
**κατάστημα με υγιεινές
τροφές** kah•_tahs_•tee•mah
meh ee•yee•ee•_nehs_ troh•_fehs_
health food store
**κατάστημα μεταχειρισμένων
ειδών** kah•_tah_•stee•mah
meh•tah•khee•reez•_meh_•nohn
ee•THohn second-hand shop
**κατάστημα αθλητικών
ειδών** kah•_tahs_•tee•mah
ath•lee•tee•_kohn_ ee•THohn
sporting goods store
κατάστημα ρούχων
kah•_tahs_•tee•mah _roo_•khohn
clothing store

κατάστημα σουβενίρ kah•_tahs_•tee•mah soo•veh•_neer_ souvenir store

κατάστημα υποδημάτων kah•_tah_•STHee•mah ee•poh•THee•_mah_•tohn shoe store

καταστρέφω kah•tah•_streh_•foh v damage

κατάψυξη kah•_tah_•psee•ksee freezer

κατεβαίνω kah•teh•_veh_•noh get off (transport)

κατειλημένος kah•tee•lee•_meh_•nohs occupied

κάτι kah•tee something

κάτοχος kah•toh•khohs owner

κατσαβίδι kah•tsah•_vee_•THee screwdriver

κατσαρόλα kah•tsah•_roh_•lah saucepan

κάτω kah•toh adj lower (berth)

καύσωνας kahf•soh•nahs heat wave

καφετέρια kah•feh•_teh_•ree•ah cafe

κέντρο της πόλης kehn•droh tees poh•lees downtown area

κεφάλι keh•_fah_•lee n head

κήπος kee•pohs n garden

κιθάρα kee•_thah_•rah guitar

κινηματογράφος kee•nee•mah•tohgh•_rah_•fohs movie theater

κίνηση kee•nee•see traffic

κινητό kee•nee•_toh_ cell phone [mobile phone BE]

κίτρινος keet•ree•nohs yellow

κλειδαριά klee•THahr•_yah_ n lock (door)

κλειδί klee•_THee_ n key

κλειδώνω klee•_THOh_•noh v lock (door)

κλειστός klees•_tohs_ adj shut

κλεμένος kleh•_meh_•nos stolen

κλέφτης klehf•tees thief

κλήση klee•see n call

κλιματισμός klee•mah•teez•_mohs_ air conditioning

κλοπή kloh•_pee_ theft

κομμωτήριο koh•moh•tee•ree•oh hair dresser

κόμβος kohm•vohs junction (intersection)

κοιμάμαι kee•_mah_•meh v sleep

κοιλάδα kee•_lah_•THah valley

κοιτάω kee•_tah_•oh v look

κολύμβηση koh•_leem_•vee•see swimming

κοντά koh•_dah_ adv near

κοντός kohn•_dohs_ adj short

κορίτσι koo•_ree_•tsee girl

κορυφή koh•ree•_fee_ n peak

κοσμηματοπωλείο kohz•mee•mah•toh•poh•_lee_•oh jeweler

κουβέρτα koo•_veh_•rtah blanket

κουζίνα koo•_zee_•nah stove

κουνούπι koo•_noo_•pee mosquito

κουρασμένος koo•rahz•_meh_•nohs tired

κουστούμι koos•_too_•mee men's suit

κουταλάκι koo•tah•_lah_•kee teaspoon

κουτάλι koo•_tah_•lee n spoon

κουτί koo•_tee_ carton

κουτί πρώτων βοηθειών koo•_tee_ proh•tohn voh•ee•THee•_ohn_ first-aid kit

κράμπα _krahm_•bah n cramp

κραγιόν krah•_yohn_ lipstick

κρατώ krah•_toh_ v keep

κρέμα ξυρίσματος _kreh_•mah ksee•_reez_•mah•tohs shaving cream

κρεμάστρα kreh•_mahs_•trah hanger

κρεβάτι kreh•_vah_•tee bed

κρυολόγημα kree•oh•_loh_•yee•mah n cold (flu)

κρύος _kree_•ohs adj cold (temperature)

κρύσταλλο _kree_•stah•loh n crystal

κύμα _kee_•mah n wave

κυλικείο kee•lee•_kee_•oh snack bar

κυλιόμενες σκάλες kee•_lee_•oh•meh•nehs skah•lehs escalator

Κύπρος _kee_•prohs Cyprus

κύριος _kee_•ree•ohs main

κωδικός περιοχής koh•THee•_kohs_ peh•ree•oh•_khees_ area code

κωπηλασία koh•pee•lah•_see_•ah rowing

Λ

λάμπα _lahm_•bah lamp, light bulb

λάθος _lah_•thohs error, wrong

λαιμόκοψη leh•_moh_•koh•psee neck (shirt)

λαιμός leh•_mohs_ throat

λάστιχο _lahs_•tee•khoh tire (tyre BE)

λειτουργία lee•toor•_yee_•ah n mass (church)

λεκές leh•_kehs_ n stain

λεξικό leh•ksee•_koh_ dictionary

λεπτό lehp•_toh_ n minute (time)

λεπτός lehp•_tohs_ adj thin

λέω _leh_•oh tell

λεωφορείο leh•oh•foh•_ree_•oh bus

ληστεία lees•_tee_•ah robbery

λιμάνι lee•_mah_•nee n harbor

λίμνη _leem_•nee lake

λιμνούλα leem•_noo_•lah n pond

λιγότερο lee•_ghoh_•teh•roh less

λιπαντικό lee•pahn•dee•_koh_ lubricant

λιπαρός lee•pah•_rohs_ greasy (hair, skin)

λιποθυμώ lee•poh•thee•_moh_ faint

λίρα _lee_•rah pound (sterling)

λίτρο _lee_•troh liter

λογαριασμός loh•ghahr•yahz•_mohs_ n check (bill), account
λοσιόν loh•_siohn_ lotion
λοσιόν μαυρίσματος loh•_siohn_ mahv•_rees_•mah•tohs sun tan lotion
λουκέτο loo•_keh_•toh padlock
λουλούδι loo•_loo_•THee n flower
λουρί ρολογιού loo•_ree_ roh•loh•_yioo_ watch strap
λόφος loh•fohs hill

Μ

μαγιό mah•_yoh_ swimming trunks, swimsuit
μαθαίνω mah•_theh_•noh learn
μάθημα ξένης γλώσσας _mah_•thee mah _kseh_•nees ghloh•sahs language course
μακιγιάζ mah•ee•_yahz_ make-up
μακριά mahk•ree•_ah_ adv far
μακρύς mak•rees adj long
μαλλιά mah•_liah_ hair
μανικιούρ mah•nee•_kioor_ manicure
μαξιλαροθήκη mah•ksee•lah•roh•_thee_•kee pillow case
μαργαριτάρι mahr•ghah•ree•_tah_•ree pearl
μάρτυρας _mahr_•tee•rahs witness
μας mahs our
μασάζ mah•_sahz_ n massage
μάσκα mahs•kah n mask (diving)
μάτι mah•tee n eye
μαχαίρι mah•_kheh_•ree knife
με meh with
με άμμο meh _ah_•moh sandy (beach)
με υπότιτλους meh ee•_poh_•teet•loos subtitled
με χαλίκια meh khah•_lee_•kiah pebbly (beach)
μεγαλοπρεπής meh•ghah•lohp•reh•_pees_ magnificent
μεγάλος meh•_ghah_•lohs adj big, large

μέγεθος _meh_•yeh•thohs n size
μέδουσα _meh_•THoo•sah jellyfish
μένω _meh_•noh v stay
μεριά mehr•_yah_ side (of road)
μερίδα meh•_ree_•THah n portion
μερικές φορές meh•ree•_kehs_ foh•_rehs_ sometimes
μέσα _meh_•sah inside
μεσημεριανό meh•see•mehr•yah•_noh_ n lunch
μετά meh•_tah_ after
μετακομίζω (μετακινώ) meh•tah•koh•_mee_•zoh v move (room)
μέταλλο _meh_•tah•loh n metal
μετάξι meh•_tah_•ksee silk
μεταφέρω meh•tah•_feh_•roh transfer
μεταφορά meh•tah•foh•_rah_ n transit
μεταφράζω meh•tah•_frah_•zoh translate
μετάφραση meh•_tah_•frah•see translation
μεταφραστής meh•tah•frah•_stees_ translator
μέτρηση _meh_•tree•see measurement
μετρητά meht•ree•_tah_ n cash
μετρό meh•_troh_ subway
μετρώ meht•_roh_ v measure
μη καπνίζοντες mee kap•_nee_•zon•des non-smoking
μήκος _mee_•kohs length
μήνας του μέλιτος _mee_•nahs too meh•lee•tohs honeymoon
μήνυμα _mee_•nee•mah n message
μηχανή mee•khah•_nee_ engine
μια φορά miah foh•_rah_ once
μικρός meek•_rohs_ little, small
μιλώ mee•loh speak
μινι-μπαρ _mee_•nee bahr mini-bar
μισός mee•_sohs_ half
μνημείο mnee•_mee_•oh memorial, monument

μολυσμένος moh•leez•_meh_•nohs infected
μονάδα moh•_nah_•THah unit
μοναδικός moh•nah•THee•_kohs_ unique
μονόκλινο δωμάτιο moh•_noh_•klee•noh THoh•_mah_•tee•oh single room
μονοπάτι moh•noh•_pah_•tee path, trail
μοντέρνος moh•_deh_•rnohs modern
μοτοποδήλατο moh•toh•poh•_THee_•lah•toh moped
μουσείο moo•_see_•oh museum
μουσική moo•see•_kee_ music
μουσικός moo•see•_kohs_ musician
μουστάκι moos•_tah_•kee moustache
μπαγιάτικος bah•_yah_•tee•kohs stale
μπάνιο _bah_•nioh bathroom, lavatory
μπαρ bahr bar
μπάσκετ _bah_•skeht basketball
μπαστούνια του σκι bahs•_too_•niah too skee ski poles
μπαταρία bah•tah•_ree_•ah battery
μπέιμπι σίτερ _beh_•ee•bee _see_•tehr babysitter
μπικίνι bee•_kee_•nee bikini
μπλούζα _bloo_•zah blouse
μπλουζάκι bloo•_zah_•kee T-shirt
μπλου-τζην bloo•_jeen_ jeans
μποξ bohks n boxing
μπότα _boh_•tah boot
μπότες πεζοπορίας _boh_•tehs peh•zoh•poh•_ree_•ahs walking boots
μπότες του σκι _boh_•tehs too skee ski boots
μπουκάλι boo•_kah_•lee bottle
μπρελόκ breh•_lohk_ key ring

μύγα _mee•ghah_ n fly (insect)
μυρίζω _mee•ree•zoh_ v smell
μυς _mees_ n muscle
μύτη _mee•tee_ n nose
μύωπας _mee•oh•pahs_ short-sighted [BE]
μωρό _mah•roh_ baby

N

ναός _nah•ohs_ temple
ναυαγοσώστης _nah•vah•ghoh•sohs•tees_ lifeguard
ναυαγοσωστική λέμβος _nah•vah•ghoh•sohs•tee•kee lehm•vohs_ lifeboat
ναυτία _nahf•tee•ah_ nausea, travel sickness
νέος _neh•ohs_ young
νερό _neh•roh_ n water
νεύρο _nehv•roh_ nerve
νεφρό _nehf•roh_ kidney
νιπτήρας _nee•ptee•rahs_ sink (bathroom)
νόμιμος _noh•mee•mohs_ legal
νομίζω _noh•mee•zoh_ think
νόμισμα _noh•meez•mah_ currency
νοικιάζω _nee•kiah•zoh_ v hire, rent
νοσοκόμα _noh•soh•koh•mah_ n nurse
νοσοκομείο _noh•soh•koh•mee•oh_ hospital
νόστιμος _nohs•tee•mohs_ delicious
Νοτιοαφρικανός _noh•tee•oh•ahf•ree•kah•nohs_ South African (nationality)
νότιος _noh•tee•ohs_ adj south
ντεμοντέ _deh•mohn•deh_ old-fashioned
ντήζελ _dee•zehl_ diesel
ντουζ _dooz_ n shower
ντουζίνα _doo•zee•nah_ dozen
νύχι _nee•khee_ n nail
νύχτα _neekh•tah_ night

νυχτερινό κέντρο _neekh•teh•ree•noh kehn•droh_ night club
νωρίς _noh•rees_ early

Ξ

ξαπλώνω _ksah•ploh•noh_ lie down
ξενάγηση _kseh•nah•yee•see_ guided tour
ξενάγηση στα αξιοθέατα _kseh•nah•yee•see stah ah•ksee•oh•theh•ah•tah_ sightseeing tour
ξεναγός _kseh•nah•ghohs_ tour guide
ξένο συνάλλαγμα _kseh•noh see•nah•lahgh•mah_ foreign currency
ξενοδοχείο _kseh•noh•THoh•khee•oh_ hotel
ξένος _kseh•nohs_ foreign
ξενώνας νεότητας _kseh•noh•nahs neh•oh•tee•tahs_ youth hostel
ξεχνώ _ksehkh•noh_ forget
ξεχωριστά _kseh•khoh•ree•stah_ separately
ξινός _ksee•nohs_ sour
ξοδεύω _ksoh•THEH•voh_ spend
ξύλο _ksee•loh_ wood (material)
ξυπνώ _kseep•noh_ v wake
ξυραφάκι _ksee•rah•fah•kee_ razor, razor blade

O

ομάδα _oh•mah•THah_ n team
όμορφος _oh•mohr•fohs_ adj beautiful, pretty
ομπρέλλα _ohm•breh•lah_ sun shade
οβάλ _oh•vahl_ oval
οδηγία _oh•THee•yee•ah_ instruction
οδηγός καταστήματος _oh•THee•ghohs kah•tahs•tee•mah•tohs_ store guide

οδηγός ψυχαγωγίας _oh•THee•ghohs psee•khah•ghoh•yee•ahs_ entertainment guide
οδηγώ _oh•THee•ghoh_ v drive
οδική βοήθεια _oh•THee•kee voh•ee•thee•ah_ road assistance
οδοντίατρος _oh•THohn•dee•aht•rohs_ dentist
οδοντόβουρτσα _oh•THohn•doh•voor•tsah_ tooth brush
οδοντόπαστα _oh•THohn•doh•pahs•tah_ tooth paste
οικογένεια _ee•koh•yeh•nee•ah_ family
οινοποιείο _ee•noh•pee•ee•oh_ winery
όνομα _oh•noh•mah_ n name
όπερα _oh•peh•rah_ opera
οπωροπωλείο _oh•poh•roh•poh•lee•oh_ greengrocer [BE]
οργανωμένος _ohr•ghah•noh•meh•nohs_ organized
ορχήστρα _ohr•khees•trah_ orchestra
οτιδήποτε _oh•tee•THee•poh•teh_ anything
οτοστόπ _oh•toh•stohp_ hitchhiking
οφείλω _oh•fee•loh_ have to (obligation)
οφθαλμίατρος _ohf•thahl•mee•aht•rohs_ optician

Π

παγοπέδιλα _pah•ghoh•peh•THee•lah_ skates
πάγος _pah•ghohs_ n ice
παιδική χαρά _peh•THee•kee khah•rah_ playground
παιδικό κρεβάτι _peh•THee•koh kreh•vah•tee_ crib [cot BE]
παίζω _peh•zoh_ v play (games, music)
παιχνίδι _pehkh•nee•THee_ n game (toy), round

παιχνίδι βίντεο pehkh•_nee_•THee vee•deh•oh video game

πακέτο pah•_keh_•toh parcel

πακέτο για το σπίτι pah•_keh_• toh yah toh _spee_•tee take away

παλιά πόλη pah•_liah_ poh•lee old town

παλιός pah•_liohs_ old (thing)

πάνα μωρού _pah_•nah moh•_roo_ diaper

Πανεπιστήμιο pah•neh•pees•_tee_•mee•oh university

πάνες μωρού _pah_•nehs moh•_roo_ nappies

πανόραμα pah•_noh_•rah•mah panorama

παντελόνι pahn•deh•_loh_•nee pants [trousers BE]

παντοπωλείο pahn•doh•poh•_lee_•oh minimart

παντόφλες pahn•_dohf_•lehs slippers

παντρεμένος pahn•dreh•_meh_•nohs married

πάνω _pah_•noh adj top, upper (berth)

παπούτσι pah•_poo_•tsee shoe

πάρα πολύ _pah_•rah poh•_lee_ too (extreme)

παραγγέλνω pah•rah•_gehl_•noh v order

παράδειγμα pah•_rah_•THeegh•mah example

παραδοσιακός pah•rah•THoh•see•ah•_kohs_ traditional

παράθυρο pah•_rah_•thee•roh window

παραλαβή αποσκευών pah•rah•lah•_vee_ ah•poh• skeh•_vohn_ baggage [BE] claim

παραλία pah•rah•_lee_•ah beach

παραλία γυμνιστών pah•rah•_lee_•ah yeem•nees•_tohn_ nudist beach

παραλυσία pah•rah•lee•_see_•ah paralysis

παράνομος pah•_rah_•noh•mohs illegal

παράξενος pah•_rah_•kseh•nohs strange

παραπάνω pah•rah•_pah_•noh more

παρεξήγηση pah•reh•_ksee_• yee•_see_ misunderstanding

πάρκο _pahr_•koh n park

παρκόμετρο pahr•_koh_•meht•roh parking meter

πάρτυ _pah_•rtee n party (social gathering)

παυσίπονο pahf•_see_•poh•noh painkiller

παχύς pah•_khees_ adj fat (person)

πέδιλα peh•THee•lah sandals

πεζόδρομος peh•_zohTH_•roh•mohs pedestrian zone

περιμένω peh•ree•_meh_•noh v hold on, wait

περιμένω στην ουρά peh•ree•_meh_•noh steen oo•_rah_ v queue [BE]

περιέχω peh•ree•_eh_•khoh contain

περιοδικό peh•ree•oh•THee•_koh_ magazine

περίοδος peh•_ree_•oh•THohs period (menstrual)

περιοχή peh•ree•oh•_khee_ region

περιοχή για καπνίζοντες peh•ree•oh•_khee_ yah kahp•_nee_•zohn•dehs smoking area

περιοχή για πικνίκ peh•ree•oh•_khee_ yah peek neek picnic area

περίπτερο peh•_ree_•pteh•roh newsstand, kiosk

περνώ pehr•_noh_ v pass

περπατώ pehr•pah•_toh_ v walk

περσίδες peh•_rsee_•THehs blinds

πετάω peh•_tah_•oh v fly

πετσέτα peh•_tseh_•tah napkin

πέφτω _pehf_•toh v fall

πηγαίνω pee•_yeh_•noh go

πιάτσα ταξί _piah_•tsah tah•_ksee_ taxi rank [BE]

πίεση pee•_eh_•see blood pressure

πιθανός pee•thah•_nohs_ possible

πινακίδα pee•nah•_kee_•THah road sign

πίνω _pee_•noh v drink

πίπα _pee_•pah pipe (smoking)

πιπίλα pee•_pee_•lah pacifier [soother BE]

πισίνα pee•_see_•nah swimming pool

πιστοποιητικό ασφάλειας pees•toh•pee•ee•tee•_koh_ ahs•_fah_•lee•ahs insurance certificate

πιστωτική κάρτα pees•toh•tee•_kee_ kahr•tah credit card

πιτσαρία pee•tsah•_ree_•ah pizzeria

πλαγιά plah•_yah_ slope (ski)

πλαστική σακούλα plahs•tee•_kee_ sah•_koo_•lah plastic bag

πλατίνα plah•_tee_•nah platinum

πλευρό plehv•_roh_ rib

πλημμύρα plee•_mee_•rah n flood

πληγή plee•_yee_ wound (cut)

πληροφορίες plee•roh•foh•_ree_•ehs information

πληρωμή plee•roh•_mee_ payment

πληρώνω plee•_roh_•noh v pay

πλοίο _plee_•oh n ship

πλυντήριο pleen•_deer_•ee•oh washing machine

πνεύμονας _pnehv_•moh•nahs lung

πόμολο _poh_•moh•loh n handle

ποδήλατο poh•_THee_•lah•toh bicycle

πόδι _poh_•THee foot, leg

ποδόσφαιρο poh•_THohs_•feh•roh soccer [football BE]

ποιότητα _pee•oh•tee•tah_ quality

πόλη _poh•lee_ town

πολυκατάστημα _poh•lee•kah•<u>tahs</u>•tee•mah_ department store

πολυτέλεια _poh•lee•<u>teh</u>•lee•ah_ luxury

πολύτιμος _poh•<u>lee</u>•tee•mohs_ valuable

πονόδοντος _poh•<u>noh</u>•THohn•dohs_ toothache

πονοκέφαλος _poh•noh•<u>keh</u>•fah•lohs_ headache

πονόλαιμος _poh•<u>noh</u>•leh•mohs_ sore throat

πόνος _poh•nohs_ n pain

πόνος στο αυτί _poh•nohs stoh ahf•<u>tee</u>_ earache

πόρτα _pohr•tah_ door

πορτοφόλι _pohr•toh•<u>foh</u>•lee_ wallet

ποσό _poh•<u>soh</u>_ n amount

ποσότητα _poh•<u>soh</u>•tee•tah_ quantity

ποταμός _poh•tah•<u>mohs</u>_ river

ποτέ _poh•<u>teh</u>_ never

ποτήρι _poh•<u>tee</u>•ree_ glass (container)

ποτό _poh•<u>toh</u>_ n drink

πουκάμισο _poo•<u>kah</u>•mee•soh_ shirt

πράσινος _prah•see•nohs_ green

πρέπει _preh•pee_ v must

πρεσβεία _prehz•<u>vee</u>•ah_ embassy

πρεσβύωπας _prehz•<u>vee</u>•oh•pahs_ long-sighted [BE]

πρήξιμο _pree•ksee•moh_ swelling

πρησμένος _preez•<u>meh</u>•nohs_ swollen

πρίζα _pree•zah_ n plug, socket

πριν _preen_ before

πρόβλεψη _prohv•leh•psee_ n forecast

πρόβλεψη καιρού _prohv•leh•psee keh•<u>roo</u>_ weather forecast

πρόβλημα _prohv•lee•mah_ problem

πρόγραμμα _prohgh•rah•mah_ n program

πρόγραμμα θεαμάτων _proh•ghrah•mah theh•ah•<u>mah</u>•tohn_ program of events

προς _prohs_ towards

προσαρμοστής _proh•sahr•moh•<u>stees</u>_ adaptor

πρόσβαση _prohz•vah•see_ n access

προσγειώνομαι _prohz•yee•<u>oh</u>•noh•meh_ v land

προσκαλώ _prohs•kah•<u>loh</u>_ v invite

πρόσκληση _prohs•klee•see_ invitation

πρόστιμο _prohs•tee•moh_ n fine (penalty)

πρόσωπο _proh•soh•poh_ n face

προσωρινός _proh•soh•ree•<u>nohs</u>_ temporary

προτείνω _proh•<u>tee</u>•noh_ v suggest

προφέρω _proh•<u>feh</u>•roh_ pronounce

προφυλακτικό _proh•fee•lah•ktee•<u>koh</u>_ condom

προωθώ _proh•oh•<u>thoh</u>_ forward

πρωί _proh•<u>ee</u>_ morning

πρωινό _proh•ee•<u>noh</u>_ breakfast

πρώτη θέση _proh•tee theh•see_ first class

πτήση _ptee•see_ flight

πυρετός _pee•reh•<u>tohs</u>_ fever

πυροσβεστήρας _pee•rohz•vehs•<u>tee</u>•rahs_ fire extinguisher

πυροσβεστική _pee•rohz•vehs•tee•<u>kee</u>_ fire brigade [BE]

πυτζάμες _pee•<u>jah</u>•mehs_ pajamas

Ρ

ραδιόφωνο _rah•THee•<u>oh</u>•foh•noh_ n radio

ρακέτα _rah•<u>keh</u>•tah_ racket (tennis, squash)

ραντεβού _rahn•deh•<u>voo</u>_ appointment

ράφι _rah•fee_ n shelf

ρεματιά _reh•mah•<u>tiah</u>_ ravine

ρεσεψιόν _reh•seh•<u>psiohn</u>_ reception (hotel)

ρεύμα ποταμού _rehv•mah poh•tah•<u>moo</u>_ rapids

ρηχή πισίνα _ree•<u>khee</u> pee•<u>see</u>•nah_ paddling pool

ρομαντικός _roh•mahn•dee•<u>kohs</u>_ romantic

ρολόι _roh•<u>loh</u>•ee_ n watch

ρυάκι _ree•<u>ah</u>•kee_ n stream

Σ

σμαράγδι _zmah•<u>rahgh</u>•THee_ emerald

σαμπουάν _sahm•poo•<u>ahn</u>_ n shampoo

σαγιονάρες _sah•yoh•<u>nah</u>•rehs_ flip-flops

σαγόνι _sah•<u>ghoh</u>•nee_ jaw

σάκκος _sah•kohs_ knapsack

σαλόνι _sah•<u>loh</u>•nee_ living room

σάουνα _sah•oo•nah_ sauna

σαπούνι _sah•<u>poo</u>•nee_ n soap

σατέν _sah•tehn_ satin

σβήνω _svee•noh_ v turn off

σβώλος _svoh•lohs_ n lump

σεζ-λονγκ _sehz lohng_ deck chair

σενιάν _seh•<u>niahn</u>_ rare (steak)

σερβιέτες _sehr•vee•<u>eh</u>•tehs_ sanitary towels

σεσουάρ _seh•soo•<u>ahr</u>_ hair dryer

σήμα _<u>see</u>•mah_ sign (road)

σημαία _see•<u>meh</u>•ah_ n flag

σημαίνω _see•<u>meh</u>•noh_ v mean

σημείο _see•<u>mee</u>•oh_ n point

σίδερο _<u>see</u>•THeh•roh_ n iron

σιδερώνω see•THeh•<u>roh</u>•noh v
iron, press

σιδηροδρομικός σταθμός
see•THeh•rohTH•roh•mee•
<u>kohs</u> stahth•<u>mohs</u> rail station

σκάλα <u>skah</u>•lah ladder

σκάλες <u>skah</u>•lehs stairs

σκηνή skee•<u>nee</u> tent

σκι skee skiing

σκιά skee•<u>ah</u> shade (darkness)

σκοπός skoh•<u>pohs</u> purpose

σκούπα <u>skoo</u>•pah n broom

σκουπίδια skoo•<u>peeTH</u>•yah trash
[rubbish BE]

σκούρος <u>skoo</u>•rohs adj dark
(color)

σλιπ sleep briefs

σόλα <u>soh</u>•lah sole (shoes)

σορτς sohrts n shorts

σουβενίρ soo•veh•<u>neer</u> souvenir

σουπερμάρκετ soo•<u>pehr</u>•
<u>mahr</u>•keht supermarket

σουτιέν soo•<u>tiehn</u> bra

σπα spah spa

σπάγγος <u>spah</u>•gohs n string (cord)

σπάνιος <u>spah</u>•nee•ohs rare
(unusual)

σπασμένος spahz•<u>meh</u>•nohs
broken

σπάω <u>spah</u>•oh v break

σπήλαιο <u>spee</u>•leh•oh n cave

σπίρτο <u>speer</u>•toh n match (to
start fire)

σπονδυλική στήλη
spohn•THee•lee•<u>kee</u> <u>stee</u>•lee
spine

σπουδάζω spoo•<u>THah</u>•zoh
v study

σταματώ stah•mah•<u>toh</u> v stop

στάδιο <u>stah</u>•THee•oh stadium

σταθμός μετρό stahth•<u>mohs</u>
meh•<u>troh</u> subway [underground
BE] station

σταθμός λεωφορείων stahTH•
<u>mohs</u> leh•oh•foh•<u>ree</u>•ohn
bus station

στάση <u>stah</u>•see exposure
(photos), stop (bus)

στάση λεωφορείου <u>stah</u>•see
leh•oh•foh•<u>ree</u>•oo bus stop

στέγη <u>steh</u>•yee n roof

στέλνω <u>stehl</u>•noh send

στενός steh•<u>nohs</u> adj narrow,
tight

στήθος <u>stee</u>•THohs breast

στόμα <u>stoh</u>•mah n mouth

στομάχι stoh•<u>mah</u>•khee n
stomach

στομαχόπονος stoh•mah•<u>khoh</u>•
poh•nohs stomach ache

στολή stoh•<u>lee</u> n uniform

στολή δύτη stoh•lee THee•tee
wetsuit

στρογγυλός strohng•gkee•<u>lohs</u>
adj round

στυλ steel n style

στυλό stee•<u>loh</u> n pen

συμπεριλαμβάνεται
seem•beh•ree•lahm•<u>vah</u>•
neh•teh included

σύζυγος <u>see</u>•zee•ghohs
husband, wife

συκώτι see•<u>koh</u>•tee liver

σύμπτωμα <u>seem</u>•ptoh•mah
symptom

συναγερμός πυρκαγιάς
see•nah•yehr•<u>mohs</u>
peer•kah•<u>yahs</u> fire alarm

συναντώ see•nahn•<u>doh</u> meet

συνέδριο see•<u>neh</u>•THree•oh
conference

συνταγή γιατρού seen•dah•<u>yee</u>
yaht•<u>roo</u> prescription

συνταγογραφώ seen•dah•
ghoh•ghrah•<u>foh</u> prescribe

συνταξιούχος seen•dah•
ksee•<u>oo</u>•khohs retired

σύντομα seen•<u>doh</u>•mah soon

συντριβάνι seen•dree•<u>vah</u>•nee
fountain

συστάσεις see•<u>stah</u>•sees
introductions

συστήνω see•<u>stee</u>•noh
introduce, recommend

συχνός seekh•<u>nohs</u> adj frequent

σφηνωμένος sfee•noh•
<u>meh</u>•nohs jammed

σφράγισμα <u>sfrah</u>•yeez•mah
filling (dental)

σφυρί sfee•<u>ree</u> hammer

σχέδιο <u>skheh</u>•THee•oh n plan

σχήμα <u>skhee</u>•mah n shape

σχισμένος skheez•<u>meh</u>•nohs
torn

σχοινί skhee•<u>nee</u> n rope

σχολή σκι skhoh•<u>lee</u> skee ski
school

σωσίβιο soh•<u>see</u>•vee•oh
lifejacket

σωστός sohs•<u>stohs</u> adj right
(correct)

Τ

ταμπόν tahm•<u>bohn</u> tampon

τάβλι <u>tah</u>•vlee backgammon

ταγιέρ tah•<u>yehr</u> women's suit

ταΐζω tah•<u>ee</u>•zoh v feed

ταινία teh•<u>nee</u>•ah movie

ταξί tah•<u>ksee</u> taxi

ταξίδι tah•<u>ksee</u>•THee journey

ταξίδι με πλοίο tah•<u>ksee</u>•THee
meh <u>plee</u>•oh boat trip

ταξιδιωτική επιταγή
tah•ksee•THee•oh•tee•<u>kee</u>
eh•pee•tah•<u>yee</u> traveler's
check [traveller's cheque BE]

ταξιδιωτικό γραφείο
tah•ksee•THyoh•tee•<u>koh</u>
ghrah•<u>fee</u>•oh travel agency

ταξιτζής tah•ksee•<u>jees</u> taxi
driver

ταυτότητα tahf•<u>toh</u>•tee•tah
identification

ταχυδρομείο tah•kheeTH•
roh•<u>mee</u>•oh post office

ταχυδρομική επιταγή
tah•kheeTH•roh•mee•<u>kee</u>
eh•pee•tah•<u>yee</u> money order

ταχυδρομικό κουτί
tah•kheeTH•roh•mee•koh
koo•tee mailbox [postbox BE]

τεμάχιο teh•mah•khee•oh
piece

τελειώνω teh•lee•oh•noh v end

τελευταί ος teh•lehf•teh•ohs
last

τελεφερίκ teh•leh•feh•reek
cablecar

τέλος teh•lohs n end

τελωνειακή δήλωση
teh•loh•nee•ah•kee
THee•loh•see customs declaration (tolls)

τελωνείο teh•loh•nee•oh
customs (tolls)

τέννις teh•nees tennis

τετράγωνος teht•rah•ghoh•
nohs square

τζετ-σκι jeht skee jet-ski

τζόγκιγκ joh•geeng jogging

τζόγος joh•ghohs gambling

τηλεκάρτα tee•leh•kahr•tah
phone card

τηλεόραση tee•leh•oh•rah•see
TV

τηλεφώνημα tee•leh•
foh•nee•mah phone call

τηλεφωνικός θάλαμος
tee•leh•foh•nee•kohs thah•
lah•mohs telephone booth

τηλεφωνικός κατάλογος tee•
leh•foh•nee•kohs kah•tah•
loh•ghohs telephone directory

τηλέφωνο tee•leh•foh•noh
n phone

την teen per

τιμή συναλλάγματος tee•mee
see•nah•lahgh•mah•tohs
exchange rate

τιμή εισόδου tee•mee
ee•soh•THoo entrance fee

τιρμπουσόν teer•boo•sohn
corkscrew

τοίχος tee•khohs wall

τοπικός toh•pee•kohs local

τοστιέρα toh•stieh•rah toaster

τουαλέτα too•ah•leh•tah
restroom [toilet BE]

τούνελ too•nehl tunnel

τουρίστας too•rees•tahs tourist

τουριστική θέση too•ree•stee•
kee theh•see economy class

τουριστικός οδηγός too•ree•
stee•kohs oh•THee•ghohs
guide book

τραβώ το καζανάκι trah•voh toh
kah•zah•nah•kee flush

τραμ trahm tram

τράπεζα trah•peh•zah bank

τραπέζι trah•peh•zee table

τραπεζομάντηλο trah•peh•
zoh•mahn•dee•loh tablecloth

τραυματισμένος trahv•mah•
teez•meh•nohs injured

τρένο treh•noh train

τρέχω treh•khoh v run, speed

τρόμπα trohm•bah n pump

τρόλλεϋ troh•leh•ee trolley-bus

τρύπα tree•pah hole (in clothes)

τρώω troh•oh v eat

τσάντα tsahn•dah handbag

τσίμπημα tsee•bee•mah n bite,
sting (insect)

τσίμπημα κουνουπιού
tseem•bee•mah koo•noo•piooh
mosquito bite

τυπικός tee•pee•kohs typical

τύχη tee•khee luck

Υ

υγρό πιάτων eegh•roh piah•tohn
dishwashing detergent

υπεραστικο λεωφορείο
ee•peh•rah•stee•koh
leh•oh•foh•ree•oh long-distance bus

υπεραστικό τηλεφώνημα
ee•peh•rah•stee•koh
tee•leh•foh•nee•mah long-distance call

υπέρβαρο ee•pehr•vah•roh
excess baggage [BE]

υπηκοότητα
ee•pee•koh•oh•tee•tah
nationality

υπηρεσία ee•pee•reh•see•ah
n service (administration,
business)

υπηρεσία δωματίου
ee•pee•reh•see•ah
THoh•mah•tee•oo room service

υπηρεσία πλυντηρίου
ee•pee•reh•see•ah
pleen•dee•ree•oo laundry
service

υπνόσακκος ee•pnoh•sah•kohs
sleeping bag

υπνωτικό χάπι
eep•noh•tee•koh khah•pee
sleeping pill

υπόγειος ee•poh•ghee•ohs
underground [BE]

υπολογιστής
ee•poh•loh•yee•stees
computer

υπόνομος ee•poh•noh•mohs
sewer

ύφασμα ee•fahs•mah fabric
(cloth)

ύψος ee•psohs height

Φ

φακός fah•kohs flashlight, lens

φακός επαφής fah•kohs
eh•pah•fees contact lens

υπηρεσία φαξ
ee•pee•reh•see•ah fahks
fax facility

φάρμα fahr•mah n farm

φάρμακα fahr•mah•kah
medication

φαρδύς fahr•THees loose
(fitting), wide

φάρος fah•rohs lighthouse

φέρνω fehr•noh bring

φέρυ-μπωτ feh•ree boht ferry

φεστιβάλ fehs•tee•_vahl_ festival
φεύγω _fehv_•ghoh v leave (depart)
φιλμ feelm n film (camera)
φίλη _fee_•lee girlfriend
φιλί fee•_lee_ n kiss
φιλοδώρημα
fee•loh•_THoh_•ree•mah gratuity
φίλος _fee_•lohs friend, boyfriend
φίλτρο _feel_•troh n filter
φιλώ fee•_loh_ v kiss
φλέβα _fleh_•vah vein
φλεγμονή flegh•moh•_nee_
inflammation
φλυτζάνι flee•_jah_•nee cup
φοβερός foh•veh•_rohs_ terrible
φοβισμένος foh•veez•_meh_•nohs
frightened
φοιτητής fee•tee•_tees_ student
φόρεμα _foh_•reh•mah n dress
φόρος _foh_•rohs duty (customs),
tax
φορώ foh•_roh_ v wear
φούρνος _foor_•nohs oven
φούρνος μικροκυμάτων
foor•nohs
mee•kroh•kee•_mah_•tohn
microwave (oven)
φούστα _foo_•stah skirt
φούτερ _foo_•tehr sweatshirt
ΦΠΑ fee•pee•_ah_ sales tax
φράγμα _frahgh_•mah n lock
(river, canal)
φράση _frah_•see n phrase
φράχτης _frahkh_•tees n fence
φρέσκος _frehs_•kohs adj fresh
φτάνω _ftah_•noh arrive
φτηνός ftee•_nohs_ cheap,
inexpensive
φτιάχνω τις βαλίτσες
ftee•_ahkh_•noh tees
vah•_lee_•tsehs v pack (baggage)
φυλακή fee•lah•_kee_ n prison
φύση _fee_•see nature
φυτό fee•_toh_ n plant

φως fohs n light (electric)
φώτα _foh_•tah lights (car)
φωτογραφία
foh•tohgh•rah•_fee_•ah v photo
φωτογραφική μηχανή
foh•tohgh•rah•fee•_kee_
mee•khah•_nee_ camera
φωτοτυπικό
foh•toh•tee•pee•_koh_
photocopier

Χ

χαμηλώνω khah•mee•_loh_•noh v
turn down (volume, heat)
χαλί khah•_lee_ rug
χαλκός khahl•_kohs_ copper
χάπι _khah_•pee tablet
χάρτης _khahr_•tees n map
χαρτί khar•_tee_ paper
χαρτί κουζίνας khahr•_tee_
koo•_zee_•nahs kitchen
χαρτί υγείας khahr•_tee_
ee•_yee_•ahs toilet paper
χαρτομάντηλο
khahr•toh•_mahn_•dee•loh tissue
χαρτομάντηλο
khah•rtoh•_mahn_•dee•loh
handkerchief
χείλη _khee_•lee lips
χειροκίνητος
khee•roh•_kee_•nee•tohs
manual (car)
χειρότερος khee•_roh_•teh•rohs
worse
χιλιόμετρα khee•_lioh_•meh•trah
mileage
χιονίζει khioh•_nee_•zee v snow
χλιαρός khlee•ah•_rohs_
lukewarm
χόμπυ _khoh_•bee hobby (pastime)
χοντρός khohn•_drohs_ thick
χορεύω khoh•_reh_•voh v dance
χορτοφάγος khohr•toh•
fah•ghohs vegetarian

χρειάζομαι khree•_ah_•zoh•meh
v need
χρέωση υπηρεσίας
khreh•oh•see ee•pee•reh•
see•ahs service charge
χρήματα _khree_•mah•tah money
χρησιμοποιώ
khree•see•moh•pee•_oh_ v use
χρήσιμος _khree_•see•mohs
useful
χρονική περίοδος
khroh•nee•_kee_ peh•_ree_•
oh•_THohs_ period (time)
χρυσός khree•_sohs_ n gold
χρώμα _khroh_•mah n color
χρωστώ khroh•_stoh_ owe
χτένα _khteh_•nah n comb
χτενίζω khteh•_nee_•zoh v comb
χτες khtehs yesterday
χώρα _khoh_•rah country (nation)
χωριό khoh•_yoh_ village
χωρίς khoh•_rees_ without
χώρος khoh•rohs n space (area)
χώρος κάμπινγκ _kah_•mpeeng
khoh•rohs campsite
χώρος στάθμευσης _khoh_•rohs
stahth•mehf•sees car park [BE]
χώρος στάθμευσης _khoh_•rohs
stahth•mehf•sees parking lot

Ψ

ψαλίδι psah•_lee_•THee scissors
ψάρεμα _psah_•reh•mah fishing
ψάχνω _psahkh_•noh look for
ψηλός psee•_lohs_ tall
ψύλλος _psee_•lohs flea

Ω

ώμος _oh_•mohs n shoulder
(anatomy)
ώρα αιχμής _oh_•rah ehkh•_mees_
rush hour
ώρες λειτουργίας _oh_•rehs lee•
toor•_yee_•ahs opening hours

INDEX

Berlitz pocket guide

CORFU

Ninth Edition 2020

Editor: Sian Marsh
Author: Donna Daily
Head of DTP and Pre-Press: Rebeka Davies
Managing Editor: Carine Tracanelli
Picture Editor: Tom Smyth and Aude Vauconsant
Layout: Aga Bylica
Cartography Update: Carte
Updated By: Marc Dubin
Photography Credits: Britta Jaschinski/Apa Publications 98, 101, 103; Corbis 89; Dr K/Wikipedia Commons 5MC; Fotolia 5TC, 77; Getty Images 6L, 43, 95; iStock 1, 4TC, 4MC, 5T, 5MC, 11, 12, 26, 28, 32, 47, 58, 69, 70, 73, 78, 86, 91, 96; Kevin Cummins/Apa Publications 4ML, 4TL, 5M, 7, 7R, 14, 18, 22, 31, 34, 39, 40, 48, 53, 54, 56, 64, 67, 75, 82, 84, 93; Paul Murphy 5M; Shutterstock 6R, 17, 37, 45, 51, 60, 63, 81; TopFoto 21
Cover Picture: Getty Images

Distribution

UK, Ireland and Europe: Apa Publications (UK) Ltd; sales@insightguides.com
United States and Canada: Ingram Publisher Services; ips@ingramcontent.com
Australia and New Zealand: Woodslane; info@woodslane.com.au
Southeast Asia: Apa Publications (SN) Pte; singaporeoffice@insightguides.com
Worldwide: Apa Publications (UK) Ltd; sales@insightguides.com

Special Sales, Content Licensing and CoPublishing
Insight Guides can be purchased in bulk quantities at discounted prices. We can create special editions, personalised jackets and corporate imprints tailored to your needs. sales@insightguides.com; www.insightguides.biz

Contact us
Every effort has been made to provide accurate information in this publication, but changes are inevitable. The publisher cannot be responsible for any resulting loss, inconvenience or injury. We would appreciate it if readers would call our attention to any errors or outdated information. We also welcome your suggestions; please contact us at: berlitz@apaguide.co.uk
www.insightguides.com/berlitz